31143011559110
641.84 Kaplan, K
Kaplan, Karen,
Open faced : DISCARDED

Main

D0116641

# OPEN FACED

Single-Slice Sandwiches from Around the World

KAREN KAPLAN

Photographs by Heidi Marie Wagstaff

**GIBBS SMITH**
TO ENRICH AND INSPIRE HUMANKIND

First Edition

21 20 19 18 17                                          5 4 3 2 1

Text © 2017 Karen Kaplan
Photographs © 2017 Heidi Marie Wagstaff

All rights reserved. No part of this book may be reproduced by any means
whatsoever without written permission from the publisher, except brief portions quoted
for purpose of review.

Published by
Gibbs Smith
P.O. Box 667
Layton, Utah 84041

1.800.835.4993 orders
www.gibbs-smith.com

Designed by Kate Frances Design
Food styling by Anni Daulter
Photographer assisted by Jessica Booth
Printed and bound in Hong Kong

Gibbs Smith books are printed on either recycled, 100% post-consumer waste,
FSC-certified papers or on paper produced from sustainable PEFC-certified forest/
controlled wood source. Learn more at www.pefc.org.

Library of Congress Cataloging-in-Publication Data
Names: Kaplan, Karen, author.
Title: Open faced : single-slice sandwiches from around the world / Karen Kaplan.
Description: First edition. | Layton, Utah : Gibbs Smith, 2017 |
Includes index.
Identifiers: LCCN 2017000302 | ISBN 9781423647430
Subjects: LCSH: Sandwiches. | Cooking, European. | LCGFT: Cookbooks.
Classification: LCC TX818 .K37 2017 | DDC 641.84--dc23
LC record available at https://lccn.loc.gov/2017000302

To my parents, Leanore and Arthur Saltz,
sans vous, rien.
Thank you for everything.

# Contents

# INTRODUCTION

I love open-faced sandwiches. They are one of my favorite forms of sustenance—so seductively elemental and essential. While I appreciate Michelin-starred haute cuisine, bistro and trattoria classics, modern gastronomy, food truck fusion, foraged whatever—the list could go on—I absolutely adore a good piece of bread topped with something tasty. The *tartines* of France, the *bruschette* and *crostini* of Italy, the *montaditos* and *pa amb* of Spain, the *smørrebrød* of Denmark, the *butterbrote* of Germany, the *molletes* of Mexico, and the toasts of America, Britain, and beyond—these are dishes that have always called to me and will always have places of honor in my culinary memory box and nostalgia file.

Today, open-faced sandwiches in all of their chef-driven, cutting-edge interpretations are the ne plus ultra of casual-chic comfort food. They are having a moment, and that moment is not going to be over any time soon, if ever. But let's get real: Open-faced sandwiches have long been part of the culinary landscapes of many countries across the globe. They speak plainly yet eloquently of their provenance—painting a picture, telling a story, and giving a history lesson in several delicious bites. They are so fundamental and popular in some countries that they constitute their own culinary category. And it is certainly easy to understand why.

Whether the sandwich is a slab of country bread grilled over an open fire, rubbed with garlic and ripe tomato, drizzled with olive oil, and sprinkled with coarse salt; or a diminutive square of pliable light rye spread with dill and lemon butter and draped with smoked salmon; or a piece of pumpernickel piled high with chopped liver, dotted with sautéed onions and hard-cooked eggs, it is sure to be eaten with gusto and appreciation. That is because very few among us can resist the undeniable pleasure and deep satisfaction that is derived from consuming an open-faced sandwich, no matter how simple or sophisticated it may be. No doubt that accounts for the longstanding adoration of these items in the countries of their origin and for their newfound prevalence in restaurants, cafés, and home kitchens.

The open-faced sandwich has been with us since the late Middle Ages, when a thick slab of coarse bread, called a *tranche* in French, or a trencher in English, was used as a plate. When the meal was over, the diner would either eat the food-soaked slice if his hunger had not been satiated, or he would give it away. It is not surprising, then, that the trencher was considered the precursor to the open-faced sandwich, not to mention tableware. While the function of the open-faced sandwich has obviously changed since the Middle Ages, the form has not. It is still, at heart, a utilitarian dish—one that uses bread as a vehicle

to transport other ingredients from the plate to the mouth, either with or without cutlery.

But whether eaten out of hand or sliced into dainty bits, this user-friendly treat is a godsend because it is a cinch to prepare, requiring a minimum of effort and a modicum of cooking. It can be put together with the most basic of ingredients from the refrigerator, pantry, or garden, and delivers maximum payoff in terms of flavor and enjoyment. It can be dressed up or dressed down, classic or creative, and can be served for breakfast, brunch, lunch, dinner, supper, or a snack. Its versatility is truly amazing, and its lusciousness cannot be denied—not to mention

it is the apogee of dinner party appetizers. All that's needed to start is some good bread.

In this book I will bring the open-faced sandwiches from several countries into the home kitchen. Some of my recipes are traditional, some are reinterpretations of classics, and some are original creations based on the flavors, ingredients, and/or specialties associated with the country at hand. Each recipe reflects the taste and spirit of its place of origin, yet is perfectly translated for the way we cook and eat in America today. This is the food I love, and I hope you will love it as much as I do. As I always say, everything tastes better on bread!

# ABOUT THE RECIPES

There are many variables in cooking, so I encourage you to look upon my recipes as flexible rather than rigid entities, and bring your common sense and personal palate into the kitchen. I want you to feel inspired, not straightjacketed.

Lots of things affect the result of a recipe: the size and thickness of a pot, pan, or skillet; the accuracy of the oven temperature; the intensity of the heat of a grill, burner, or cooktop; the way you cut something; and even your own individual taste buds. So when I tell you to cook an onion over medium heat until it is softened, and that it will take about 10 minutes to do so, please keep in mind that your skillet and your stove are probably different from mine, or those of the tester, so the time is approximate. If your onion is softened at 8 minutes, you are done; if your onion

needs more than 10 minutes, well, cook it more. If I tell you to season something generously with salt and pepper, and you don't like a lot of salt and pepper, then season it lightly with salt and pepper. If I tell you to add hot sauce, and you hate hot sauce, don't add it. At the end of the day, it's up to you. And remember to taste as you go. If I call for the juice of 1 lemon, but you want more, add more!

In addition, since everything in this book is served on bread, and bread slices vary in size, you may end up having more topping than bread or more bread than topping. If that happens, not to worry: just make an extra sandwich or pile more topping on each bread slice. If you want to use a different bread from the one I call for, that's cool; if you want to use gluten-free bread, that's dandy, too; and if you don't want to use bread at all, that's just fine—crackers or just a plate will work well for many of these recipes. If I call for the bread to be toasted but you don't want it toasted, don't toast it, and vice versa.

At this point it goes without saying, but I will say it anyway: the better the ingredients that go into a recipe, the better the outcome. So always try to use the best ingredients you can find and afford. But don't make yourself crazy. Sometimes whatever you have on hand is completely acceptable. I don't call for too many exotic ingredients in this book, but whenever I do, I offer substitutes, so none of these recipes should be out of reach to anyone. And if you need to cut a recipe in half, or double or triple it, that's fine too.

# INSTANT OPEN-FACED SANDWICHES

This is a cookbook filled with recipes for open-faced sandwiches. So it may seem counterintuitive and/or a bit masochistic to tell you that you do not need a recipe to make an easy open-faced sandwich with international flair, but that is indeed the truth. I know that you don't always have time to cook from a recipe; I certainly don't. Sometimes you just want to slap something together with what you have on hand, and that's fine. So here are some open-faced sandwich tips for the days when you just don't have time to make a recipe—even one of my fabulous recipes.

### Bread and Cured Meat
A slice of good bread or toast slathered with butter or drizzled with olive oil and topped with salami, prosciutto, speck, jamón, Bayonne ham, saucisson, or whatever cured meat your heart desires is an unbeatable combination. If mustard is your thing, go for it. Serve with some olives and wine, and you have a meal of the gods.

### Bread and Cheese
### (except for mozzarella, burrata, and ricotta)
A slice of good bread or toast is at its simple and sexy best when topped or spread with yummy cheese. Your yummy cheese may not be my yummy cheese, but that's not the point: the point is that the cheese be of fine quality, no matter what kind it is. Could there be a better meal on the run?

If you are a fan of fruit with your cheese, you can't go wrong with thin slices of apples, pears, figs, persimmons, or even grapes or cherries arranged over or under the cheese. Dried fruit works well, too, as does the miraculous quince paste.

If you are a fan of cheese and jam, why not try cheese with jam? Trust me, it is fantastic. I love cheddar and marmalade, Brie with cherry jam, Camembert with apricot jam, Gorgonzola with fig jam, and the list goes on. And in a similar sweet vein, there is not a blue cheese alive that does not like honey. Why not experiment with different pairings?

### Bread and Cured Meat and Cheese

A slice of good bread or toast is the perfect place to stack cured meat and cheese, if that is your wont. You can complement the combo with butter, mustard, jam, or fruit depending on what you have put together. It's hard to resist ham and cheddar, or Brie and prosciutto, or salami and Parmesan, or whatever kind of double trouble you love best.

### Bread, Meat and/or Cheese . . . and all those condiments you forgot about

A slice of good bread or toast is the perfect place to unload all those pestos, tapenades, savory jams, spreads, and relishes that you've been collecting in your cupboard. Eat them on their own or top them with cured meat or cheese—or both—and you will be happy.

### Bread with Mozzarella or Burrata

A slice of good bread or toast topped with slices of mozzarella or burrata, drizzled with fantastic extra virgin olive oil and aged balsamic vinegar, and seasoned with salt and pepper is heavenly, but I wouldn't say no to the addition of cured meat, pesto, tapenade, roasted peppers, sun-dried tomatoes, or fresh tomato slices. No sweet jam or honey, though.

### Bread with Ricotta Cheese

A slice of good bread or toast mounded with fresh whole-milk ricotta cheese, drizzled with olive oil, and sprinkled with salt and pepper is also celestial. But ricotta is such a good foil for so many things. Go savory with sun-dried tomatoes, roasted peppers, grilled or sautéed vegetables, or shredded fresh vegetables. Or go sweet with fresh or dried fruit, jam, honey, syrup, peanut or almond butter, or Nutella. Go crunchy with nuts, seeds, granola, chocolate chips, or cacao nibs.

### Bread and Tomato

A slice of good bread or toast with slices of ripe tomato is an essential combination. Some people insist on slathering the bread with mayonnaise, others drizzling it with olive oil, but everyone can agree on salt. When tomatoes are in season, that is the way to go. You may want to gild the lily with cured meat, cheese, tuna, sardines, or anchovies, but purists may balk.

### Bread and Smoked Salmon

A slice of good bread or toast spread with butter or crème fraîche and draped with smoked salmon is hard to top. You can leave it at that, or gussy things up with capers, onions, chopped egg, and/or caviar.

### Bread with Just About Anything

I am of the mind that almost everything tastes better on bread. While clearly that is not entirely true, you get my drift. So when you are looking for an instant open-faced sandwich, let your imagination—as well as your pantry and refrigerator—be your guide. Greens such as spinach, arugula and watercress, mesclun, and basil add a fresh bite to almost any sandwich, and romaine lettuce is always good for crunch. And don't forget, leftovers are terrific!

# TARTINES

## ⬦⬦⬦⬦⬦⬦⬦⬦⬦⬦⬦⬦⬦⬦⬦ FRANCE ⬦⬦⬦⬦⬦⬦⬦⬦⬦⬦⬦⬦⬦⬦⬦

A *tartine* refers to a piece of untoasted bread topped with something sweet or savory. (The linguistic origin of the word is the French verb *tartiner*, which means "to spread.") When it is sweet, it is usually served for breakfast or a snack—a length of baguette slathered with butter and jam is a morning staple, and a piece of bread with butter and chocolate is a traditional after-school treat for kids. But when it is savory, it is usually lunch, especially these days with French people—particularly young French people—opting for lighter midday fare. You would be hard-pressed to find a café anywhere in France that didn't offer at least a few savory tartines. And those are the kinds I will concentrate on here.

Lunchtime tartines can be as basic as a piece of bread spread with butter and covered with ham, or something much more complicated indeed. These midday tartines are often on bread other than a baguette, usually something that resembles *pain Poilâne,* the famous two-kilo sourdough country bread, also referred to as *miche.* The bread is made of stone-ground wheat and spelt flour, fermented naturally, and baked in a wood-fired oven. But a tartine is a flexible and fluid creation, and you can pretty much use whatever bread you want and whatever toppings, as long as they are of superior quality.

There are restaurants around the world that have taken the name La Tartine and specialize in both traditional and up-to-the minute versions of the French café staple, and certainly the upscale Belgian café chain Le Pain Quotidien has made an art out of the open-faced sandwich. But tartines are super simple to make at home, and a lovely treat for absolutely any time of day at all.

# THE BREAD

In Paris, the bread most often used for savory tartines comes from the bakery company Poilâne. It is a handcrafted round loaf weighing approximately four pounds and is comprised of four ingredients: naturally fermented sourdough starter, stone-ground wheat flour, water, and sea salt. Called *pain au levain*, or miche, it is cooked in a wood-burning oven and comes out with a very thick crust, spongy yet taut interior, and distinctive and addictive tangy taste. Because of the shape of the round, the slices are perfect for tartines: the largest ones from the center, which measure approximately 11 inches long and $4\,^1/_2$ inches wide, are usually cut in half, each half being the perfect size for one tartine. Obviously as you move away from the center of the loaf, the slices get smaller, at which point whole rather than half slices must be used. The slices are generally $^1/_4$ to $^1/_3$ inch thick, which is fine because this is one sturdy bread. The bread is available by mail order and in some upscale markets. You can find an excellent similar bread, also called pain au levain, at Le Pain Quotidien, a Belgian chain of organic cafes and bakeries located all over the world, including in many cities in the United States. (If you buy a whole or half round, make sure you have them slice it for you.) Trader Joe's has a knockoff loaf they call Pain Pauline, which is available in a half round, and while the size and taste are similar to Pain Poilâne, the texture is more crumbly.

While this kind of bread is optimum for tartines, slices from any large, round loaf of country bread will do, whether white, sourdough, wheat, or multigrain. A dense, firm interior texture is a must, however, in order to hold the toppings. Some of my recipes call for the bread to be toasted; you can grill, broil, or toast your bread according to your preference.

# Boursin, Roquette, and Radish

MAKES 4 TARTINES

The world's first variety of Boursin—the classic Garlic and Fine Herbs—was created in 1957 in Normandy by none other than François Boursin. His inspiration came from a traditional French dish for which dinner guests are offered a bowl of *fromage frais* (fresh cheese, like ricotta) and bowls of fines herbes (fresh chervil, parsley, chives, and tarragon) to mix together as they like. The resulting Boursin cheese became the first flavored cheese to be sold in France. While Boursin does not normally grace a refined after-dinner cheese board, it is creamy, tangy, delicious, and popular around the world. As a bonus, it makes a wonderful base for a tartine. This one is so easy, topped with *roquette* (the French word for arugula, or rocket as it is called in Britain), radishes, and chives. A lighter, minerally, high-acid wine such as Chablis or Sancerre pairs perfectly with this dish.

4 tartine bread slices (see page 13)

1 Boursin Garlic and Fine Herbs cheese, quartered

4 small handfuls arugula

4 large radishes, very thinly sliced

Extra virgin olive oil, for drizzling

Coarse salt

1 bunch chives, snipped, for garnish

Arrange bread on a platter or individual plates. Spread each with 1 quarter of cheese and top with a handful of arugula, pressing into cheese to hold in place. Arrange a quarter of the radish slices atop arugula on each slice, overlapping if necessary. Drizzle with olive oil. Sprinkle with salt. Garnish with chives and serve.

# Lentil and Sausage Salad

## MAKES 4 TARTINES

This classic French bistro salad tastes just as good on bread as it does on a plate. I like to use the tiny, tender du Puy lentils from France, which hold their shape extremely well, but feel free to use any kind of lentil you like, adjusting the cooking time accordingly. If you would like to make this salad vegetarian, use cubes of Gruyère cheese instead of sausage; if you would like to make it vegan, use tofu instead of sausage or cheese. A great wine to pour with this is a younger, lighter Malbec- or Cabernet-based red from the hinterlands of Bordeaux such as Cahors or Bergerac.

$^1/_2$ cup small French du Puy lentils, picked over, rinsed, and drained

2 small carrots, peeled, 1 halved crosswise and 1 diced

2 small celery stalks, 1 halved crosswise and 1 diced

1 small onion, halved

1 large garlic clove, peeled

1 thyme sprig

1 bay leaf

4 ounces cooked smoked garlic sausage, such as kielbasa, diced

1 tablespoon red wine vinegar

1 teaspoon Dijon mustard

$^1/_4$ cup olive oil

Salt and freshly ground black pepper

1 small shallot, minced

4 tartine bread slices (see page 13)

Chopped fresh flat-leaf parsley, for garnish

Combine lentils, carrot and celery halves, onion, garlic, thyme, and bay leaf in a pot. Add enough cold water to cover ingredients by 2 inches and bring to a boil. Reduce heat and simmer gently, uncovered, until lentils are tender, about 20 minutes; time will vary depending on size and age of lentils. Drain lentils, discard vegetables and herbs, and cool completely. (Can be prepared 1 day ahead. Cover and refrigerate. Bring to room temperature before continuing.)

Meanwhile, place sausage in a small, heavy skillet over medium heat and sauté until fat is rendered and sausage is crisp and browned. Using a slotted utensil, transfer sausage to a paper towel to drain.

Whisk vinegar and mustard in a bowl. Drizzle in the oil in a steady stream and whisk until emulsion forms. Season vinaigrette generously with salt and pepper.

Transfer lentils to a bowl. Stir in the diced carrot and celery, sausage, and shallot. Add vinaigrette and toss well. Season salad generously with salt and pepper.

Grill, broil, or toast the bread. Arrange toasts on a platter or individual plates. Divide salad evenly among toasts. Garnish with parsley and serve.

# Flageolet Beans, Roast Lamb, and Shallots

## MAKES 6 TARTINES

Small, light-green flageolet beans are called the caviar of beans. They are almost never available fresh, even in France, and are most typically served alongside roast lamb. You can buy them dried or canned. If you cannot find them, use canned navy, cannellini, or great Northern beans instead. Uncork a southern red Rhône wine such as Gigondas, or a named Côte-du-Rhône village such as Rasteau or Cairanne.

1 (1- to 1 1/4-pound) lamb leg steak

6 garlic cloves, minced

6 thyme sprigs, leaves finely chopped

3 rosemary sprigs, leaves finely chopped

2 anchovy fillets, finely chopped

3/4 cup plus 1 tablespoon olive oil, divided

1 lemon, halved

Salt and freshly ground black pepper

1 (14.11-ounce) can cooked flageolet beans, rinsed and drained

8 shallots, halved and thinly sliced

6 tartine bread slices (see page 13)

Grated lemon peel, for garnish

Coarse salt, for garnish

Place lamb in a large ziplock bag. Combine garlic, thyme, rosemary, and anchovy fillets in a small bowl. Whisk in 5 tablespoons olive oil. Squeeze in juice from lemon halves and whisk to blend. Season with salt and pepper. Pour marinade over lamb and work into meat. Refrigerate for at least 1 hour or up to overnight.

Place beans in a processor and pulse to a coarse purée. With machine running, stream in 5 tablespoons oil and purée until smooth. Transfer to a bowl and season with salt and pepper. Let stand until ready to use. (Can be prepared 1 day ahead. Cover and refrigerate. Bring to room temperature before using.)

Heat 2 tablespoons oil in small, heavy skillet over medium-high heat. Add shallots and cook until crisp, stirring frequently, about 10 minutes. Season with salt and pepper. Let stand until ready to use.

Preheat oven to 400 degrees. Heat 1 tablespoon oil in a medium-size heavy ovenproof skillet over medium-high heat. Remove lamb from ziplock, allowing liquid to drip back into bag. Brown lamb very well on first side, turn over, and repeat on second side; do not rush the process. Roast in skillet to desired doneness, about 5 minutes for medium rare and 10 minutes for medium. Transfer meat to a cutting board and let stand for at least 10 minutes. Using a sharp knife, cut lamb into thin slices.

Grill, broil, or toast the bread. Arrange toasts on a platter or individual plates. Spread evenly with bean purée and top with slices of lamb. Garnish with frizzled shallots, lemon peel, and coarse salt and serve.

# Ratatouille

Ratatouille is a classic French Provençal sautéed vegetable dish. While it originated in Nice, it is now popular along the entire Mediterranean coast and, indeed, throughout much of France. It is usually served room temperature and is most commonly a side dish at dinner, though one can find it in crepes, omelets, and on its own. Legend has it that the word *ratatouille* is the love child of two French verbs—*ratouiller* and *tatouiller*—expressive forms of the French verb *touiller*, which means "to stir up." Cooking the vegetables separately is a bit time consuming but yields a traditionally superior final product. Also, this is a beautiful do-ahead dish, as it actually tastes better the next day . . . or the next! These vegetables are also delicious tossed with pasta. This calls for a younger Côtes-du-Rhône or other earthy Grenache-based wine from the south of France.

6 tablespoons olive oil, divided

1 pound ripe tomatoes, chopped

4 large garlic cloves, minced

4 thyme sprigs

Pinch of sugar

Salt and freshly ground black pepper

2 onions, diced

2 red bell peppers, diced

1 small eggplant, diced

3 medium zucchini, diced

1 teaspoon herbes de Provence

8 tartine bread slices (see page 13)

Extra virgin olive oil, for drizzling

Coarse salt, for sprinkling

Freshly grated Parmesan cheese, for garnish

Chopped fresh basil, for garnish

Heat 2 tablespoons oil in a medium-size heavy skillet over medium heat. Add tomatoes, garlic, thyme, and sugar and cook until a thick sauce forms, stirring occasionally, about 20 minutes. Discard thyme sprigs. Season with salt and pepper. Set tomato sauce aside.

Meanwhile, heat 2 tablespoons oil in a large, heavy skillet over medium heat. Add onions and bell peppers and sauté until tender but not browned, about 20 minutes. Transfer to another large, heavy skillet. Heat 1 tablespoon oil in original skillet. Add eggplant and sauté until cooked through, about 20 minutes. Transfer to skillet with onions and peppers. Heat remaining 1 tablespoon oil in original skillet. Add zucchini and sauté until cooked through, about 10 minutes. Transfer to skillet with onions, peppers, and eggplant. Add tomato sauce and mix well. Cook over medium-low heat to meld flavors, stirring occasionally, about 5 minutes. Remove from heat. Stir in herbes de Provence. Season generously with salt and pepper. Transfer to a bowl and let cool to room temperature. (Can be made several days ahead. Cover and refrigerate. Bring to room temperature before serving.)

Grill, broil, or toast the bread. Arrange toasts on a platter or individual plates. Divide ratatouille evenly among toasts. Drizzle with oil and sprinkle with coarse salt. Garnish with Parmesan and basil.

# Anchoïade, Roasted Bell Peppers, Goat Cheese, and Basil

Anchoïade is a classic Provençal dip or spread. As anchovies are the stars of the show, you have to love them to love this tartine. (If you want to take a bit of the bite out of the little fishies, you can soak them in milk or water for 10 minutes before using.) And an affinity for garlic doesn't hurt either! I've paired the spread with other yummy Provençal ingredients, including roasted red peppers, goat cheese, and basil. While it is easy enough to roast your own peppers, directions for which I have provided here, you can certainly purchase a jar of roasted peppers instead. Your best beverage bet to complement both the anchovies and the goat cheese is a Loire Sancerre or Pouilly-Fumé, a Provençal rosé, or, yes, believe it or not, Champagne.

3 (2-ounce) tins oil-packed anchovies, drained

3 medium garlic cloves, chopped

2 tablespoons (1/4 stick) butter, room temperature

1 tablespoon red wine vinegar

1/4 (or more) cup olive oil

Freshly ground black pepper

2 large red, yellow, and/or orange bell peppers

6 tartine bread slices (see page 13)

1 cup crumbled fresh goat cheese

12 large basil leaves, cut into chiffonade, for garnish

Place anchovies and garlic in a mini food processor or blender and process to a paste. Add butter and process until smooth. (You can use a full-size processor; if you do, make sure to scrape down sides of bowl regularly.) Transfer mixture to a bowl. Whisk in the vinegar. Whisk in 1/4 cup oil in a steady stream to form a thick spread, whisking in more oil if too thick. Cover and refrigerate anchoïde until ready to use. (Can be prepared 1 day ahead. Bring just to room temperature before using.)

Heat broiler to high and arrange rack in upper third of oven. Place bell peppers on rack and broil until blackened and blistered on all sides, turning occasionally, about 20 minutes. Alternatively, roast peppers on the grill or over an open stove burner flame until blackened and blistered on all sides. Immediately transfer peppers to a heatproof bowl. Cover tightly with plastic wrap and let stand for 15 minutes. When peppers are cool enough to handle, peel and/or rub off blackened skins. Remove cores, seeds, and membranes and cut peppers into strips. (Can be prepared 1 day ahead. Cover and refrigerate. Bring to room temperature before using.)

Grill, broil, or toast the bread. Arrange toasts on a platter or individual plates. Spread each toast generously with anchoïde. Top with pepper strips then goat cheese, dividing evenly. Garnish with basil and serve.

# Potatoes, Bayonne Ham, and Raclette Cheese

MAKES 4 TARTINES

Raclette is a semi-hard cow's milk cheese that dates from medieval times. It was originally consumed by cow herders in mountainous Switzerland and the French region of Savoie, and remains popular with the Swiss and French to this day. Cow herders would eat the cheese as is during the day, but come nightfall they would place it next to a campfire, and when it had melted, they would scrape it atop bread (*racler* means "to scrape" in French). That simple act has evolved into a famous dish, also called raclette, in which a half wheel of the cheese is placed on a special stand in front of an open fire and scraped onto a plate as it melts. The cheese is served with country bread, boiled potatoes, cured meats, cornichons, and sometimes little pickled white onions. Here I've put everything on a tartine.

Raclette is easy to find in cheese stores and supermarkets with fine cheese sections. If you cannot find it, you can use Gruyère, Comté, Emmentaler, Appenzeller, or Morbier instead. Delectable dry-cured Bayonne ham from the Basque region in the southwest of France is a quintessential French ingredient. Look for it at specialty food stores, or use prosciutto instead. Pour a Bourgogne Rouge if you can spring for it; otherwise a Cru Beaujolais such as Chiroubles, Fleurie, Morgon, or Brouilly will do nicely.

4 small Yukon gold potatoes, peeled and cut into $1/4$-inch-thick slices

4 tartine bread slices (see page 13)

4 teaspoons Dijon mustard

8 thin slices Bayonne ham or prosciutto

Salt and freshly ground black pepper

$1/2$ pound raclette cheese, trimmed and thinly sliced

Cornichons, for serving

Pickled baby white onions, for serving

Place potatoes in a pot. Cover with cold water. Bring to boil and cook until tender; do not overcook. Drain.

Preheat broiler. Arrange bread on a baking sheet. Spread each slice with 1 teaspoon mustard, top with 2 slices of ham, and arrange $1/4$ of the potato slices over each. Season with salt and pepper. Cover each with slices of raclette. Broil until raclette melts.

Transfer tartines to a platter or individual plates. Serve immediately with cornichons and pickled onions atop or alongside.

# Sautéed Belgian Endive, Blue Cheese, Walnuts, and Honey

MAKES 4 TARTINES

Belgian endive did indeed originate in Belgium in the nineteenth century, but it is now popular just about everywhere, especially in France, where its slightly bitter flavor is beloved both fresh and cooked. A common French salad is one of chopped Belgian endive, crumbled blue cheese, and walnuts, and those flavors shine here, though the endive is sautéed so it's easier to pile on toast. I call for a French blue because this is, after all, a tartine, but any kind of blue cheese works well here, particularly if you prefer your blue a little less pungent. But the drizzle of honey complements the strong flavors of the endive and cheese beautifully. To drink, try a younger demi-sec Vouvray or another slightly sweet wine with good acid, such as a German Riesling Kabinett.

2 tablespoons (¹/4 stick) butter

2 tablespoons olive oil

4 shallots, halved and thinly sliced

6 heads Belgian endive, slivered crosswise, cores discarded

Salt and freshly ground black pepper

1 small bunch flat-leaf parsley, finely chopped

4 tartine bread slices (see page 13)

¹/4 pound Roquefort cheese, Fourme d'Ambert, Bleu d'Auvergne, Saint Agur, or any fine blue cheese, crumbled

4 teaspoons (or more) honey

¹/4 cup chopped walnuts, toasted

Melt butter with oil in a large, heavy skillet over medium heat. Add shallots and sauté until softened and starting to brown, about 5 minutes. Add endive and sauté until wilted and tender, about 10 minutes. Season generously with salt and pepper. Let cool slightly. Stir in parsley.

Preheat broiler. Arrange bread on a baking sheet. Divide endive mixture evenly among bread slices. Sprinkle each evenly with cheese. Drizzle each with 1 teaspoon honey, adding more if desired. Broil until cheese bubbles and melts. Transfer tartines to a platter or individual plates. Garnish with walnuts and serve.

# Roasted Bone Marrow with Pickled Red Onions and Watercress

MAKES 4 TARTINES

Bone marrow is beloved in France and chefs often place a disc of it atop a steak, or whisk it into a sauce for extra richness. But perhaps it is at its best just roasted and spread on toast. All animal bones have marrow in them, but when you're talking roasted bone marrow, you're usually talking about the femur bones of beef cows. These bones are simple to roast and eat because they are straight, wide, and offer lots of easy-to-access marrow. Buy them at a reputable butcher shop and get the butcher to split them vertically for you. Roasted bone marrow doesn't need much more than lots of salt and pepper, but pickled red onions and watercress add a refreshing contrast of flavor and texture. No watercress? Use spinach leaves or arugula instead. If you're a vegetarian or just don't like bone marrow, never fear. Spread your bread with goat cheese and top with the onions and watercress. When all else fails, Champagne comes to the rescue, and it is *parfait* here.

1 large red onion, thinly sliced

1 cup warm water

$^1/_2$ cup apple cider vinegar

1 tablespoon sugar

$^1/_2$ tablespoon coarse salt

2 large marrow bones, split vertically

Olive oil, for drizzling

Salt and freshly ground black pepper

4 tartine bread slices (see page 13)

1 bunch watercress, thin stems and
  leaves only

Place onion in a small glass bowl. Whisk water, vinegar, sugar, and $^1/_2$ tablespoon salt together in another bowl; make sure sugar and salt dissolve. Pour the mixture over the onion. Let stand at room temperature for at least 1 hour. (Can be made up to 2 weeks ahead. Cover and refrigerate. Bring to room temperature before using.) Drain onion.

Preheat oven to 450 degrees. Line a baking sheet with aluminum foil. Set marrow bones cut side up on foil. Drizzle lightly with oil. Season with salt and pepper. Roast until bubbling and heated through, about 20 minutes.

Meanwhile, grill, broil, or toast the bread. Arrange toasts on a platter or individual plates. Spread marrow from 1 marrow bone half onto each toast. Season with salt and pepper. Top toasts with watercress and drained pickled onions. Serve immediately.

# Provençal Tuna and Vegetable Salad

## MAKES 4 TARTINES

This is a takeoff on pan bagnat, a sandwich that is a street food specialty of Nice and beloved throughout Provence and, indeed, all of France. It means "wet bread" in a combination of the French and Occitan languages, and has long been prepared as a way to use up day-old bread. Pan bagnat is essentially a country roll filled with something similar to salad Niçoise. Needless to say, my version is open-faced! If you want to splurge, get premium tuna packed in oil—it's delicious. The wine choice is obvious here: a chilled bottle of really good Provençal rosé.

1 (5- or 6-ounce) can tuna, drained

1 Persian or Kirby cucumber, minced

1 small or $^1/_2$ large green, yellow, or orange bell pepper, minced

$^1/_2$ small red onion, minced

2 large radishes, minced

2 generous tablespoons chopped oil-cured black and/or green olives

1 tablespoon red wine vinegar

1 teaspoon Dijon mustard

2 small garlic cloves, minced

$^1/_4$ cup olive oil

Salt and freshly ground black pepper

4 tartine bread slices (see page 13)

2 plum tomatoes, thinly sliced

2 hard-boiled eggs, thinly sliced

8 anchovy fillets (optional)

Extra virgin olive oil, for drizzling

Chopped fresh basil, for garnish

Combine tuna, cucumber, bell pepper, onion, radishes, and olives in a medium bowl. Whisk together the vinegar, mustard, and garlic in a small bowl. Whisk in the oil in a steady stream. Pour over tuna salad. Season generously with salt and pepper.

Arrange bread slices on a platter or individual plates. Divide tuna salad among bread slices. Divide tomatoes and eggs evenly among tartines, arranging decoratively. Crisscross 2 anchovy filets over each tartine if desired. Drizzle with extra virgin olive oil. Garnish with basil and serve.

# Creamy Leeks with Cremini and Chanterelle Mushrooms

MAKES 6 TARTINES

While there are many varieties of chanterelles, the most popular is golden chanterelles. With their seductive color, meaty texture, and distinctive fruity flavor, they are a mushroom lover's dream. These seasonal 'shrooms don't come cheap, but a little of them goes a long way. Make sure to treat your delicious investment with care: clean the chanterelles well with a mushroom brush or damp paper towel; do not, under any circumstances, soak them in water. Here I have mixed the chanterelles with the more affordable and readily available cremini mushrooms. If you cannot find chanterelles, or you do not want to use them, just use cremini mushrooms exclusively. The delicate flavor of leeks complements the mushrooms beautifully. Splurge on a lovely Bourgogne Blanc if you can afford it, or a semi-serious Mâcon if you cannot. Either way, you will be happy.

8 tablespoons (1 stick) butter, divided

4 leeks, white and light-green parts only, cleaned well, halved, and thinly sliced

$1/2$ cup dry white vermouth or dry white wine

2 cups heavy cream

2 tablespoons olive oil

10 ounces cremini mushrooms, thinly sliced

$1/4$ pound chanterelle mushrooms, halved if small or sliced if large

Salt and freshly ground black pepper

3 tablespoons minced fresh thyme leaves, divided

4 tartine bread slices (see page 13)

Melt 3 tablespoons butter in a large, heavy skillet over medium heat. Add leeks and sauté until softened, about 10 minutes. Add vermouth and cook until almost evaporated. Add cream and bring just to a boil. Reduce heat and simmer very gently until leeks are tender and cream is thick, stirring occasionally, about 10 minutes.

Meanwhile, melt remaining 5 tablespoons butter with oil in a large, heavy skillet over medium-high heat. Add both mushrooms and sauté until browned and juices have been released and reabsorbed, about 10 minutes. Add mushrooms to leek mixture and mix well. Season generously with salt and pepper. Stir in 1 tablespoon thyme leaves.

Grill, broil, or toast the bread. Arrange toasts on a platter or individual plates. Divide leek and mushroom mixture evenly among toasts. Garnish with remaining 2 tablespoons thyme leaves. Serve immediately.

# BRUSCHETTE AND CROSTINI

Wasting bread is considered a *pecato*, or sin, in Italy, as it is in many other countries in Europe. What better way to make use of a loaf that is past its prime than to cut it into slices, grill those slices, top them with something savory, and serve them as an appetizer? *Ecco* bruschette and crostini! And while the kinds of bread and toppings may change from region to region in Italy, the idea and the template remain the same.

Bruschette and crostini have gone from complete obscurity to domination of the dining table, first in authentic Italian restaurants, and now, well, just about everywhere. But let's not get them confused. Bruschette, from the Italian verb *bruscare*, which means "to roast over coals," refers to large pieces of rustic bread that are grilled, sometimes rubbed with garlic, and then topped. Crostini, which means "little toasts," refers to smaller, thinner slices of more refined bread that are toasted and then topped. While still hearty, crostini are definitely more delicate than bruschette.

But whether referring to a bruschetta (singular) or bruschette (plural), a crostino (singular) or crostini (plural), you are actually referring to the bread and not the toppings, which means that you have to describe the toppings so people know what they are eating. In any case, both bruschette and crostini are considered an antipasto, or appetizer, though they seem to have morphed to serve other purposes in some Western countries.

Because bruschette and crostini are, at heart and at their very best, extremely simple constructions, you must use the best ingredients possible for the best results. But that goes without saying, now doesn't it?

# THE BREAD

## Bruschette

To make bruschette, you need a large round loaf or thick oval loaf of rustic bread, preferably Italian or French in style, with a firm, thick crust and a firm interior consistency. To be authentic, select one made with white flour or a mixed flour blend, but if you prefer sourdough, wheat, or multigrain—go for it. To be perfectly honest, I generally use the sourdough boule from Trader Joe's and find that the slices cut from the center are the perfect size for my recipes, not to mention the bread is delicious, has a great texture, and grills up beautifully.

Use a good bread knife to cut the loaf into as many ½-inch-thick slices as you need for your recipe, but if you like your slices a bit thinner, not to worry. Just don't make them too thin, or they will fall apart under the weight of the topping. At this point you should also peel some garlic cloves, the number of which will vary depending on the size of the cloves and how many slices of bread you have, but let's say you need one medium clove of garlic for every two slices of bread. Also have some olive oil and salt ready.

There are several options for grilling the bread—and some do not involve grilling at all—depending on what is available to you. You can grill it over an open fire; on a wood, charcoal, or gas grill; or on a stovetop grill pan. Alternatively, you can toast it under the broiler or in a toaster oven. If worst comes to worst, give it a long plunge in the toaster, or plonk it right on top of your burner (but be careful and don't have the heat too high). The key is to get the bread crispy with perhaps some burnt edges—I actually like my bread quite crisp. You do not want flabby bread, as it cannot stand up to the toppings. Remember, the bread is acting like an edible plate.

As soon as the bread is grilled, you will want to transfer it to a cutting board and rub the surface of the bread with garlic. Then drizzle the bread ever-so-gently with olive oil and season it with salt. The bruschette are now ready to be used in whichever recipe you might choose. (If for some reason you would like to skip the garlic, oil, and salt part, the bread will still work in the recipe.)

## Crostini

To make crostini, you will need an Italian or French baguette. Once again, white is most traditional, but go for sourdough, wheat, or multigrain if that is your preference. Cut off the ends of the baguette and eat or discard them. Cut the remaining baguette on the diagonal into ¼- to ⅓-inch-thick slices. Arrange the slices on a baking sheet (or sheets if necessary) and drizzle or brush the tops of the slices lightly with olive oil. Bake in a preheated 400 degree oven until the bread turns golden brown, about 10 minutes. Rub with garlic if desired. You can make these several days in advance. Let them cool completely and store at room temperature.

# Tomato, Garlic, and Basil

## MAKES 4 BRUSCHETTE

This is the one that started the bruschette/crostini craze. It's simple, delicious, and everyone loves it. I prefer to serve it as a sit-down, knife-and-fork first course for an Italian meal. You can spice things up with the addition of capers and/or chopped black or green olives. I like to make this a few hours ahead so the flavors can marry, but you can make it and serve it right away in a pinch. Uncork a light-bodied Chianti from the Tuscan area of Rufina.

1 pound cherry tomatoes, halved if small or quartered if large

2 medium garlic cloves, minced

Salt and freshly ground black pepper

$^1/_4$ cup extra virgin olive oil

$^3/_4$ cup torn or chopped fresh basil leaves

4 bruschette (see page 31)

Place tomatoes and garlic in a bowl. Season generously with salt and pepper. Stir in olive oil. Cover and let stand at room temperature for 2 to 3 hours; do not refrigerate.

Right before serving, season mixture again with salt and pepper. Stir in basil leaves. Arrange bruschette on a platter or individual plates. Spoon tomato mixture over each bruschetta, permitting excess to fall onto the platter or plate. Serve immediately.

# Prosciutto, Pecorino Romano-Roasted Asparagus, and Gremolata

## MAKES 6 BRUSCHETTE

This is a beautiful stand-alone dish and a splendid appetizer as well. Prosciutto is a beloved Italian dry-cured ham, the best of which is made in Parma in Emilia-Romagna, and San Daniele in Friuli. Pecorino Romano has a similar texture to that of Parmesan but a saltier flavor. Production of the cheese is allowed only on Sardinia, in the region of Lazio, and in the Tuscan province of Grosseto. Both prosciutto and Pecorino Romano are easy to find at Italian delis and most supermarkets. Gremolata is a parsley, lemon peel, and garlic condiment traditionally used as a garnish on the Milanese veal shank dish osso buco, but it works perfectly here. Two white wines from opposite ends of the Italian peninsula would be fabulous with this: Arneis from Piedmont and Fiano di Avellino from Campania.

24 medium-thick asparagus spears (about 1 bunch), woody ends trimmed

2 tablespoons olive oil

$1/2$ teaspoon coarse salt

$1/4$ teaspoon freshly ground black pepper

2 tablespoons grated Pecorino Romano cheese, plus more for garnish

1 bunch flat-leaf Italian parsley, leaves only, finely chopped

3 large garlic cloves, minced

1 tablespoon grated lemon peel

12 thin slices prosciutto

6 bruschette (see page 31)

Preheat oven to 425 degrees.

Arrange asparagus in a single layer on a baking sheet. Drizzle with olive oil and sprinkle with salt and pepper. Roll asparagus around to coat completely. Sprinkle with 2 tablespoons cheese and roll again to coat completely. Roast until asparagus are tender but not mushy, about 15 minutes; time will vary depending on thickness of asparagus.

Meanwhile, combine parsley, garlic, and lemon peel in small bowl. Season with salt and pepper. Set aside.

Arrange bruschette on a platter or individual plates. Top each bruschetta with 2 prosciutto slices. Lay 4 asparagus spears atop prosciutto on each bruschetta. Garnish with gremolata and additional Pecorino Romano cheese if desired. Serve immediately.

# Fava Bean Purée with Sautéed Escarole

Fresh fava beans are one of the great joys of spring, but they have a very, very short season, so here I call for frozen or canned favas, lima beans, or edamame as a substitute. This bruschetta is a take on a classic dish from the region of Puglia called *Purée di Fave e Cicoria*, which is essentially dried fava bean purée served with slow-cooked bitter greens. If you haven't tried it, you don't know what you're missing. But you can get an idea here! Uncork a crisp, minerally Verdicchio di Matelica with this sandwich.

1 cup frozen shelled and skinned fava beans, lima beans, or edamame, thawed, or canned fava beans, drained and rinsed

4 medium garlic cloves, chopped, divided

10 tablespoons olive oil, divided

1 tablespoon fresh lemon juice

1 teaspoon minced fresh rosemary

Salt and freshly ground black pepper

2 bunches escarole, trimmed, cored, and leaves finely chopped

6 bruschette (see page 31)

Extra virgin olive oil, for drizzling

Coarse salt, for sprinkling

Place fava beans in a food processor. Add a quarter of the chopped garlic and purée. With machine running, stream in 6 tablespoons olive oil in a steady stream. Blend in lemon juice. Blend in rosemary. Season with salt and pepper. Spoon into a bowl, cover, and let stand until ready to use. (Can be prepared 1 day ahead and refrigerated. Bring to room temperature before using.)

Heat remaining 4 tablespoons olive oil in a large, heavy skillet over medium heat. Add remaining chopped garlic and sauté until fragrant, about 30 seconds. Add escarole and sauté until wilted and tender, about 10 minutes. Season with salt and pepper.

Arrange bruschette on a platter or individual plates. Divide fava bean purée among bruschette. Top with sautéed escarole. Drizzle with extra virgin olive oil, sprinkle with coarse salt, and serve.

# Dried Fig Jam, Pancetta, and Gorgonzola Dolce

## MAKES 6 BRUSCHETTE

Fresh figs and prosciutto is a classic Italian combination, but here I have changed things up a bit by pairing a dried fig jam with pancetta, an unsmoked pork belly cured in salt and spices that comes in a rolled shape. The original sweet and salty marriage is still in play, and since fresh figs aren't always in season, you can make this sandwich all year long! I have added some Gorgonzola Dolce (also known as Dolcelatte) to gild the lily. This mild, buttery, blue-veined cow's milk cheese from Lombardy is the lesser-aged sibling of the stronger and more crumbly Gorgonzola Piccante (also known as Gorgonzola Naturale). Both the pancetta and the cheese are available at Italian delis and most supermarkets. I can't imagine a better match for this than Moscato d'Asti. PS: You will probably have a bit of jam leftover; no worries, it is delicious on your breakfast toast!

1 cup chopped dried black mission figs, hard ends snipped

1 cup (or more) water

2 tablespoons honey, preferably Italian

1 tablespoon balsamic vinegar

2 teaspoons fresh lemon juice

Salt

12 very thin slices pancetta

6 bruschette (see page 31)

12 thin slices Gorgonzola Dolce (sweet Gorgonzola) or Castello blue cheese

Place figs and water in a small, heavy saucepan over medium-high heat and bring to a boil. Reduce heat to low and simmer until figs are plump and very soft, about 20 minutes. (If too much water evaporates, add just enough additional water to keeps figs simmering.) Cool mixture slightly.

Transfer mixture to a food processor. Add honey, vinegar, and lemon juice and purée until the consistency of paste. Season to taste with salt. Cool jam to room temperature before using. (Can be prepared 3 days ahead. Cover and refrigerate. Bring to room temperature before using.)

Preheat broiler. Arrange pancetta slices in single layer on a broiler pan or baking sheet. Broil until just crispy and slightly curled.

Arrange bruschette on a platter or individual plates. Spread each with a thick layer of dried fig jam. Top each with 2 pancetta slices and 2 cheese slices, pressing down, and serve.

# Peperonata and Ricotta Salata

## MAKES 6 BRUSCHETTE

I fell in love with peperonata, an Italian condiment of stewed onions, peppers, and a bit of tomato, when I spent time on the glorious Tuscan island of Elba. There it seems to be served with just about everything. It is delicious hot, room temperature, or cold, so take your pick! I love this with a sprinkling of ricotta salata—the firm, salty, and crumbly version of its fresher sibling. It is made from the whey part of sheep's milk and then pressed, salted, and aged for at least ninety days. It is available at some supermarkets and most Italian delis; if you cannot find it, you can use feta cheese. A number of mineral-driven, medium-bodied Italian whites would work well here, including Soave, Verdicchio, and Falanghina.

1/4 cup olive oil

3 bell peppers (red, orange, and/or yellow; no green), cored, veined, seeded, and thinly sliced

3 onions, halved and thinly sliced

4 large garlic cloves, chopped

1 cup tomato sauce

2 oregano sprigs

Salt and freshly ground black pepper

6 bruschette (see page 31)*

Extra virgin olive oil, for drizzling

3/4 cup crumbled ricotta salata cheese

2 tablespoons minced fresh oregano

Heat 1/4 cup oil in a Dutch oven or large, heavy pot over medium heat. Add peppers, onions, and garlic and cook until beginning to soften, stirring frequently, about 20 minutes. Stir in tomato sauce and oregano sprigs. Reduce heat and simmer until peppers and onions are very soft, stirring occasionally, about 1 hour.

Remove and discard oregano sprigs. Season peperonata generously with salt and pepper. (Can be made 2 days ahead. Cool completely, cover, and refrigerate until ready to use. Bring to room temperature or reheat if desired.)

Arrange bruschette on a platter or individual plates. Divide peperonata evenly among bruschette. Drizzle with extra virgin olive oil. Divide cheese evenly among bruschette, pressing into the peperonata. Sprinkle with minced oregano and serve.

*If you prefer this as cocktail party finger-food crostini (as shown in the photo), use smaller pieces of bread (see page 31).*

# Sautéed Radicchio, Speck, and Mozzarella

### MAKES 4 BRUSCHETTE

Speck is a prize product of the mountainous Alto Adige region in the very north of Italy, bordering Austria and Switzerland. It is a distinctly flavored smoked, cured ham that is more robust in taste than the sweet, subtle prosciutto produced in San Daniele in the region of Friuli, and Parma in the region of Emilia-Romagna. It is available at Italian delis, some supermarkets, and by mail order. If you cannot find it, you can use prosciutto. The smokiness of the speck and the creaminess of the mozzarella marry deliciously with sautéed radicchio, the bitterness of the beloved Italian chicory tamed by some balsamic vinegar and brown sugar. Choose a medium-bodied Italian red such as Barbera d'Alba or Barbera d'Asti, Chianti, Rosso di Montalcino, or Montepulciano d'Abruzzo to accompany this bruschetta.

2 tablespoons olive oil

1 red onion, thinly sliced

3 garlic cloves, minced

1 large head radicchio, halved, cored, and thinly sliced

Salt and freshly ground black pepper

2 tablespoons balsamic vinegar

1 tablespoon brown sugar

4 bruschette (see page 31)

8 thin slices speck

8 slices fresh mozzarella cheese, patted dry

2 tablespoons minced fresh basil, for garnish

Heat oil in a medium-size heavy skillet over medium heat. Add onion and sauté until softened, about 10 minutes. Add garlic and sauté until fragrant, about 30 seconds. Add radicchio, season with salt and pepper, and sauté until radicchio is almost wilted, about 5 minutes. Stir in vinegar and brown sugar and cook until radicchio is completely wilted, dark in color, and all liquid is absorbed, stirring frequently, about 15 minutes. Adjust seasoning with salt and pepper.

Arrange bruschette on a baking sheet. Divide radicchio mixture among bruschette. Top each with 2 pieces of speck then 2 pieces of mozzarella. Broil until cheese melts. Transfer bruschette to a platter or individual plates. Garnish with basil and serve immediately.

# Arugula, Bresaola, Parmesan, and Oven-Roasted Tomatoes

## MAKES 4 BRUSCHETTE

Bresaola is air-dried, salted top inside round of beef that has been aged two or three months. It originated in Valtellina, a valley in the Alps of northern Italy's Lombardy region. It is usually served as an antipasto, sliced thin and drizzled with olive oil, balsamic vinegar, or lemon juice and served with shavings of Parmesan cheese and an arugula salad. (If you cannot find bresaola, prosciutto is also delicious.) Here I combine all three on a bruschetta and add juicy and flavorful oven-roasted tomatoes. The tomatoes are terrific on any sandwich and tossed with pasta as well. I use a cheese shaver to get large shavings from a big wedge of Parmesan cheese. If you purchase pre-shaved Parmesan, in which the pieces are smaller, you will probably need to use more—enough to cover the sandwich. Serve with a slightly fruity Italian white such as Pinot Grigio or Müller-Thurgau.

16 Roma or plum tomatoes

5 tablespoons olive oil, divided

2 tablespoons balsamic vinegar

2 teaspoons sugar

Salt and freshly ground black pepper

8 large garlic cloves, thinly sliced

2 large rosemary sprigs

2 large thyme sprigs

2 large oregano sprigs

4 handfuls arugula (about 3 ounces)

1 tablespoon fresh lemon juice

4 bruschette (see page 31)*

8 thin slices bresaola

16 large shavings Parmesan cheese

Preheat oven to 350 degrees. Slice core ends off tomatoes. Cut tomatoes in half vertically and remove cores and seeds. Place tomatoes on a baking sheet. Drizzle with 4 tablespoons oil and the vinegar. Sprinkle with sugar. Season with salt and pepper. Scatter garlic slices atop tomatoes. Using a spatula or clean hands, toss tomatoes to coat well. Arrange tomatoes cut side down, top with herb sprigs, and roast until tomatoes are withered and caramelized, about 30 minutes. Using tongs, transfer tomatoes from the sheet to a platter and let cool.

Place arugula in a bowl. Toss with remaining 1 tablespoon oil and the lemon juice. Season with salt and pepper. Arrange bruschette on a platter or individual plates. Press 4 roasted tomato halves into each bruschetta. Top each with a quarter of the arugula and cover with 2 bresaola slices and 4 Parmesan shavings. Top each bruschetta with 4 roasted tomato halves, or serve the remaining tomatoes on the side for guests to top as they please.

*If you prefer this as cocktail party finger-food crostini (as shown in the photo), use smaller pieces of bread (see page 31).*

# Sautéed Mushrooms and Taleggio Cheese

MAKES 20 TO 25 CROSTINI

Italians love their mushrooms and their cheese, so it's natural for them to combine the two on a crostino. Taleggio is a washed-rind, cave-aged, tangy, and very delicious semi-soft cow's milk cheese from Lombardy. Once almost impossible to find outside of Italian delis and fine cheese stores, Taleggio is now making an appearance in some supermarkets with well-sourced cheese departments. It melts lusciously and marries beautifully with the earthy mushrooms. If you cannot find Taleggio, try real Italian fontina or Robiola. To drink, let's keep things in Lombardy with a subtle Nebbiolo of the Valtellina, such as a Valtellina Superiore or Grumello.

3 tablespoons butter

3 tablespoons olive oil

3 shallots, minced

3 garlic cloves, minced

1 $^1/_2$ pounds cremini mushrooms, stemmed and very thinly sliced

2 tablespoons minced fresh thyme, plus more for garnish

1 baguette, sliced diagonally and baked into crostini (see page 31)

20–25 (1 $^1/_2$ x 1-inch) pieces Taleggio cheese without rind (about $^1/_3$ pound total)

Melt butter with oil in large, heavy skillet over medium heat. Add shallots and sauté until translucent, about 5 minutes. Add garlic and sauté until fragrant, about 30 seconds. Increase heat to medium-high. Add mushrooms and sauté until browned and all liquid has been released and reabsorbed, 8 to 10 minutes. Stir in 2 tablespoons thyme.

Preheat broiler. Arrange crostini on a baking sheet. Pack sautéed mushrooms evenly atop each crostino and top with 1 piece of Taleggio cheese. Broil until cheese melts. Arrange crostini on a platter. Garnish with fresh thyme. Serve immediately.

# White Bean Purée with Roasted Garlic, Herbs, and Fried Sage Leaves

MAKES 30 TO 35 CROSTINI

White beans are an Italian favorite, especially in Tuscany, where the people of the region are often called *mangiafagioli* (bean eaters) because of their penchant for the ingredient. Simmered white beans are a typical side dish; white bean salad is a lovely appetizer or lunch dish; and a simple purée slathered on toast is a customary crostini. This recipe actually makes enough for a baguette and a half's worth of crostini, so if you only want to do one baguette, slather generously, or save the leftovers for another use. This spread is great on sandwiches or as a dip for veggies. This calls for a fine, full-bodied Pinot Grigio from the northeastern Italian region of Friuli. Or if you prefer to stay in Tuscany, look for a Vernaccia di San Gimignano.

1 medium to large garlic head

1/4 cup olive oil, plus more for drizzling and frying

Salt and freshly ground black pepper

3 tablespoons mixed chopped fresh herbs, such as sage, parsley, oregano, marjoram, rosemary, thyme, and/or chives

2 (15-ounce) cans cannellini or great Northern beans, drained and rinsed

2 tablespoons fresh lemon juice

30–35 sage leaves, washed and patted dry

1 1/2 baguettes, sliced diagonally and baked into crostini (see page 31)

Preheat oven to 400 degrees. Peel or rub away topmost layers of skin on the garlic head, leaving skins of individual cloves intact. Cut off the top of the head, exposing tops of cloves. Set garlic head in a garlic roaster or on a sheet of aluminum foil. Drizzle with oil. Season with salt and pepper. Place cover over garlic in roaster or seal garlic head completely in foil. Roast until fragrant and cloves are very soft, about 45 minutes; time will vary depending on size of garlic head.

Let garlic cool. Squeeze cloves into a food processor; discard skins. Add herbs and pulse to combine. Using a spatula, scrape down sides of the processor bowl. Add beans, 1/4 cup oil, and lemon juice; purée until almost smooth. Season generously with salt and pepper. Transfer to a bowl.

Pour 1/4 inch of oil into a medium-size heavy skillet and heat over medium-high heat until hot but not smoking. Add sage leaves and fry until crisp and dark green, 2 to 3 minutes per side. Transfer to a paper towel. Sprinkle with salt.

Arrange crostini on a platter. Spread each generously with bean purée. Place 1 fried sage leaf atop each. Serve immediately.

# Sautéed Sausage and Four Cheeses

## MAKES 20 TO 25 CROSTINI

This is one of the simplest and most satisfying crostino there is. You need very few ingredients and very little time to throw together an appetizer that is sure to please. I buy the Quattro Formaggi (four cheese) mix (asiago, Parmesan, fontina, and mild provolone) at Trader Joe's, but it is also sold at other stores. Of course, you can use any kind or combination of grated Italian cheeses you want, though not mozzarella as it is too stringy. Almost any Italian red would complement this treat, so choose your favorite: one of mine is Montefalco Rosso from Umbria. PS: If you use chicken or turkey sausage, you will probably have to add more oil to the skillet.

1 tablespoon olive oil

1 pound sweet or spicy Italian sausages

1 small onion, minced

4 garlic cloves, minced

1 tablespoon minced fresh oregano, or 1 teaspoon dried, crumbled

1 baguette, sliced diagonally and baked into crostini (see page 31)

1 cup grated four cheese blend

Minced fresh oregano, for garnish

Heat oil in a medium-size heavy skillet over medium heat. Remove sausage from casings and place sausage in skillet; discard casings. Cook sausage until cooked through, breaking up meat with a wooden spoon or pressing meat with a potato masher if finer texture is desired. Using a slotted utensil, transfer sausage to a bowl, leaving rendered fat in the skillet. Pour off all but 1 tablespoon fat from the skillet. (If not enough fat has been rendered, add olive oil to make up the difference.) Add onion and sauté until softened, about 10 minutes. Add garlic and sauté until fragrant, about 30 seconds. Transfer onion and garlic to the sausage and mix well. Add 1 tablespoon oregano and mix well.

Preheat broiler. Arrange crostini on baking sheets. Add cheese to the sausage mixture and toss well. Mound mixture onto each crostino. Broil until cheese melts. Transfer to a platter, sprinkle with fresh oregano, and serve immediately.

# Herbed Ricotta and Sautéed Zucchini with Lemon

## MAKES 20 TO 25 CROSTINI

Herbed ricotta makes a good base for just about anything, and it is used as such on many bruschette and crostini, but it is especially delicious topped with sautéed zucchini. I like to cook my zucchini until it is crisp and browned, and I think you will too! Feel free to change up the herb here. If you prefer thyme or oregano or even mint, go for it. Pour a lighter-bodied, younger Italian red such as Lagrein from Alto Adige or Dolcetto from Piedmont.

1 $1/2$ cups whole-milk ricotta cheese, drained if watery

1 bunch chives, minced

$1/3$ cup finely chopped fresh basil

3 tablespoons olive oil, divided

3 teaspoons grated lemon peel, divided

Salt and freshly ground black pepper

4 garlic cloves, chopped

2 medium zucchini, cut into very small dice

1 baguette, sliced diagonally and baked into crostini (see page 31)

Coarse salt, for sprinkling

Combine ricotta, chives, basil, 1 tablespoon oil, and 1 teaspoon lemon peel in a bowl. Season with salt and pepper. Set aside until ready to use. (Can be prepared several hours ahead. Cover and refrigerate. Bring to room temperature before using.)

Heat remaining 2 tablespoons oil in a large, heavy skillet over low heat. Add garlic and sauté until fragrant, about 30 seconds. Increase heat to medium. Add zucchini and sauté until crisp and golden brown, about 10 minutes. Season with salt and pepper.

Arrange crostini on a platter. Spread ricotta mixture evenly over each. Top with sautéed zucchini, sprinkle with coarse salt and remaining lemon peel, and serve.

# Three Flavors

## MAKES 60 TO 75 CROSTINI

Italian bruschette or crostini are often smeared with some kind of spread, traditionally olivada (olive spread) and sometimes basil pesto or sun-dried tomato pesto. I have provided you with those three recipes here, but do not feel obliged to make them all at once. Each recipe makes about 1 cup, which is more than enough for crostini made from one baguette. Keep in mind that these spreads are easy to make, keep well, and have many other uses—try them tossed with pasta or vegetables, or slathered on a pizza or sandwich. Pair these delights with the famous Italian white wine, Soave.

3 baguettes, sliced diagonally and baked into crostini (see page 31)

Place Basil and Arugula Pesto, Sun-Dried Tomato Pesto, and Olivada (recipes below) in bowls. Arrange crostini on a platter and serve.

## Basil and Arugula Pesto

1 cup firmly packed basil leaves
1 cup firmly packed arugula leaves
$^1/_4$ cup toasted pine nuts
2 garlic cloves
$^1/_3$ cup olive oil, plus more for covering pesto
$^1/_2$ cup grated Parmesan cheese
Salt and freshly ground black pepper

Place basil, arugula, pine nuts, and garlic in a food processor and pulse to coarsely purée. With machine running, stream in half of the $^1/_3$ cup oil. Stop and scrape down sides of processor bowl. Add cheese and pulse to blend well. With machine running, stream in remainder of the $^1/_3$ cup oil. Season with salt and pepper. Transfer to a bowl. Cover with a thin film of oil. Let stand at room temperature until ready to use. (Can be made several days ahead. Cover and refrigerate. Bring to room temperature before using.)

*Continued >*

## Sun-Dried Tomato Pesto

1 cup oil-packed sun-dried tomatoes
  (about 8.5 ounces), drained

$1/4$ cup olive oil

1 cup firmly packed basil leaves

2 garlic cloves

$1/4$ cup grated Parmesan cheese

Salt and freshly ground black pepper

Combine tomatoes, oil, basil, garlic, and Parmesan in a food processor and purée. Season with salt and pepper. (Can be made several days ahead. Cover and refrigerate. Bring to room temperature before using.)

## Olivada

1 cup pitted brine-cured black
  and/or green olives

1 tablespoon red wine vinegar

$1/3$ cup olive oil

1 tablespoon capers, drained and
  rinsed

3 garlic cloves

$1/4$ teaspoon crushed red pepper

Salt and freshly ground black pepper

Combine olives, vinegar, oil, capers, garlic, and red pepper in a food processor and pulse to desired consistency. Season with salt and pepper. (Can be made several days ahead. Cover and refrigerate. Bring to room temperature before using.)

# Caponata

## MAKES 20 TO 25 CROSTINI

This Sicilian staple is thought to have originated long ago as a dish for sailors to take on their voyages, as it kept well because of the vinegar. But no matter how the specialty got started, it has been going ever since, and its fame has reached far beyond Sicily. The sweet-and-sour notes of this versatile creation, which has numerous regional variations, is typical of Sicily, where myriad culinary influences come into play, including Greek, Spanish, French, and Arab. Sometimes a bit of unsweetened cocoa powder is added for richness; sometimes it is garnished with toasted almonds or slices of hard-boiled eggs. Feel free to play with your food, or just to make it as is. Pour an aromatic white Greco di Tufo from Campania or Greco di Bianco from Calabria, or if you want to go Sicilian, look for a Grillo, Catarratto, or Inzolia.

1 pound eggplant (about 1 medium), cut into ¹/₂-inch cubes

Salt

6 tablespoons olive oil, divided

2 large celery stalks, chopped

1 onion, chopped

3 large garlic cloves, chopped

³/₄ cup tomato sauce

¹/₂ cup chopped pitted Sicilian green olives, or other Mediterranean green olives

2 tablespoons capers, drained and rinsed

1 ¹/₂ tablespoons sugar

¹/₄ cup white wine vinegar

Salt and freshly ground black pepper

Flat-leaf Italian parsley leaves, for garnish

1 baguette, sliced diagonally and baked into crostini (see page 31)

Place eggplant cubes in a colander. Sprinkle generously with salt. Let stand in sink for 1 hour. Pat eggplant dry; do not rinse.

Heat 2 tablespoons oil in a large, heavy skillet over medium heat. Add celery and onion and cook until softened and golden brown, stirring frequently, about 15 minutes. Add garlic and stir until fragrant, about 30 seconds. Add tomato sauce, olives, capers, sugar, and vinegar and simmer until thickened, about 15 minutes.

Meanwhile, heat remaining 4 tablespoons oil until very hot but not smoking in another large, heavy skillet over medium-high heat. Add eggplant cubes in a single layer and cook until browned and crisp, about 5 minutes; flip eggplant cubes over and cook until browned and crisp on second side, about 5 minutes. Transfer eggplant to sauce in the other skillet. Cool to room temperature. Season caponata with salt and pepper. (Can be prepared 3 days in advance. Cover and refrigerate. Bring to room temperature before using.)

Transfer caponata to a serving bowl and garnish with parsley leaves. Arrange crostini on a platter and serve alongside the caponata.

# MONTADITOS AND TOMATO TOASTS

## ◇◇◇◇◇◇◇◇◇◇◇◇◇◇◇◇ SPAIN ◇◇◇◇◇◇◇◇◇◇◇◇◇◇◇◇

*Montaditos* are a staple of Spanish tapas bars and have been around since the fifteenth century. These decorative open-faced sandwiches, which are typically bite-sized but can also be more substantial, delight the eye and the palate. They are always made with fabulous Spanish ingredients such as jamón (cured ham), Manchego cheese, chorizo, piquillo peppers, anchovies, sardines, quince paste, and shrimp, just to mention a few. These toppings are "riding" on a small slice of baguette, which makes sense given that montar means "to mount" and usually refers to mounting a horse. Montaditos can be hot or cold and are perfect for cocktail parties or as a dinner party hors d'oeuvre, especially accompanied by flutes or coupes of sparkling Spanish wine, known as cava. In the Basque country, montaditos are called *pintxos* in Euskara, the Basque language, or *pinchos* in Spanish.

In Catalunya (Catalonia) and the Balearic Islands (Mallorca, or Majorca, Minorca, Ibiza, and Formentera), the classic bread with savory topping is toasted *pa*, or bread, rubbed with garlic and tomato. The pieces of bread are definitely not bite-sized and have nothing to do with montaditos. Called *pa amb tomàquet* in Catalan, *pan con tomate* or *tostada* in Spanish, and tomato toast in English, it has become ubiquitous around Spain and, in fact, on menus in many a fashionable restaurant all over the world. Often it is topped with anchovies or jamón, or accompanied by a plate of one or the other alongside. In its place of origin, it is eaten for breakfast, a snack, tapas, or as an appetizer. Sometimes simplicity is sublime, and pa amb tomáquet proves the point, no matter where, when, or how it is served.

# THE BREAD

Traditional montaditos are typically made with slices of bread that come from a Spanish loaf similar to a baguette, but larger; those slices are sometimes toasted and sometimes not. The slices do, in fact, resemble crostini, though they are often bigger. So in my recipes for montaditos that call for smallish slices of toasted bread, I refer you to my directions for making the bread for crostini (page 31).

However, in the majority of my recipes, I call for larger, thicker slices from a bigger loaf of bread as they just work better with the toppings. (I probably shouldn't call the sandwiches montaditos, as that is a diminutive linguistic form, but what the heck.) The bread slices for these should come from a large round or thick oval loaf of rustic bread, whether white, sourdough, wheat, or multigrain. You can grill, broil, or toast them according to your preference.

The *pa amb*, or toasts, from Catalunya, are their own special category, and always use large, thick slices of country bread.

# Mallorcan Tomato Toasts

## MAKES 4 TOASTS

On the stunning Catalunyan island of Mallorca, pa amb tomàquet is transformed into something completely different by using sliced tomatoes and a piquant garnish of a mix of olives, capers, and herbs. Called *pamboli amb tomàtiga* in the Mallorcan language, it is absolutely delicious on its own or as a base for anchovies, jamón, cheese, or just about anything else. If you are a wine sleuth, see if you can find a white or rosé from Mallorca; otherwise, try one or the other from Rioja.

4 large, thick slices country bread

4 juicy tomatoes (preferably vine-ripened)

Extra virgin olive oil (preferably Spanish), for drizzling

Coarse salt

$1/2$ cup chopped pitted oil-cured black olives

$1/2$ cup chopped fresh flat-leaf parsley

3 tablespoons rinsed and drained capers, minced

2 tablespoons minced fresh thyme leaves

Grill, broil, or toast bread. Arrange toasts on a platter or individual plates. Using a very sharp or serrated knife, cut tomatoes into paper-thin slices. Discard core and end pieces. Arrange tomato slices from 1 tomato across surface of each toast, overlapping if necessary. Using a spatula, press tomato slices into toast to release juices into bread. Drizzle with oil and sprinkle with salt. Mix olives, parsley, capers, and thyme in a small bowl. Divide mixture among toasts, spooning over tomatoes, and serve.

# Catalan Tomato Toasts

## MAKES 4 TOASTS

The northeastern Spanish region of Catalunya, which borders France and the Mediterranean Sea and includes the islands of Mallorca, Minorca, Formentera, and Ibiza, is renowned for its food and wine. Perhaps its most famous dish is its simplest: pa amb tomàquet—grilled bread rubbed with garlic and tomato then drizzled with olive oil and sprinkled with salt. It is absolutely luscious and the perfect foil for a host of toppings, most commonly anchovies, slices of Jamón Serrano (dry-cured ham), or cheese, but really, almost anything tastes good on it. Traditionally the bread is rubbed on both sides, but that can get a bit messy, so even many Catalans just go for one side, as I have here. Look for a dry white wine from the Catalunyan wine-producing region of Penedès, or the white Txakolina from the Basque country. A dry rosé from Rioja would also be delicious.

4 large, thick slices country bread

2 large garlic cloves, halved

2 juicy tomatoes (preferably vine-ripened), halved crosswise

Extra virgin olive oil (preferably Spanish), for drizzling

Coarse salt

Grill, broil, or toast bread. Transfer toasts to a work surface. Rub each piece of toast with 1 garlic clove half. Rub each piece of toast with 1 tomato half, gently squeezing to leave a thin red film including some seeds, flesh, and juice. Arrange toasts on a platter or individual plates. Drizzle each toast with oil, sprinkle with salt, and serve.

# Piperrada

MAKES 6 MONTADITOS

This lovely dish of scrambled eggs with peppers, tomatoes, and Serrano ham is a typical Basque dish that is served for breakfast, lunch, or even as an accompaniment to grilled or roasted meats at dinner. I love it piled high on toasts—perfect for a quick brunch, supper, or protein-filled snack. The garnish of grated P'tit Basque cheese—one of my favorites—is completely inauthentic, but I love the little burst of sweet, nutty flavor it adds. This sheep's milk cheese is produced in the French Pyrénées Mountains, which span the border between France and Spain. It is available at cheese stores, of course, but also at stores like Trader Joe's, Costco, and most supermarkets that have a decent cheese section. Believe it or not, a chilled lager or lighter ale would be perfect with this dish.

4 tablespoons olive oil, divided

1 small onion, finely chopped

1 small red bell pepper, finely chopped

1 small green bell pepper, finely chopped

3 garlic cloves, minced

6 thin slices Jamón Serrano or prosciutto, finely chopped

2 small tomatoes, finely chopped

Salt and freshly ground black pepper

6 eggs

6 large, thick slices country bread

6 tablespoons grated P'tit Basque cheese

6 tablespoons finely chopped fresh cilantro

Heat 2 tablespoons of oil in a large, heavy skillet over medium heat. Add onion and bell peppers and sauté until softened, about 5 minutes. Add garlic and sauté until fragrant, about 30 seconds. Add Jamón Serrano and sauté for 1 minute. Add tomatoes, season with salt and pepper, and cook until vegetables are tender and mixture thickens, stirring occasionally, about 10 minutes. Let cool slightly. (Can be prepared 1 day ahead. Cover and refrigerate. Bring to room temperature before using.)

Crack eggs into a bowl and beat well with a fork or whisk. Stir vegetable and ham mixture into eggs. Wipe out skillet. Heat remaining 2 tablespoons oil in same skillet over medium-low heat. Add egg mixture and cook, stirring constantly, until eggs are set but not dry.

Grill, broil, or toast bread. Arrange toasts on a platter or individual plates. Divide egg mixture evenly among toasts. Sprinkle each with 1 tablespoon cheese and 1 tablespoon cilantro and serve immediately.

# Chickpeas, Spinach, and Chorizo

## MAKES 20 TO 25 MONTADITOS

Spinach is a particular favorite in the large southernmost region of Andalucía (Andalusia), and at tapas bars there, especially in Seville, you will often find a dish of spinach and chickpeas. Here I have added some chorizo for extra flavor. Remember that Spanish chorizo and Mexican chorizo are different. While they are both pork sausages, Mexican chorizo is sold uncooked and is usually removed from its casing, while Spanish chorizo is sold cooked and can be sliced and eaten as you would salami, or it can be heated up. Make sure you buy Spanish chorizo for this dish; whether you buy sweet or spicy is up to you. (If you cannot find it, you can use a sausage such as kielbasa.) I flavor this dish with pimentón, Spanish paprika, and once again, choose sweet or spicy according to your taste. Since chickpeas are devilish creatures, threatening to roll off the bread at every bite, I call for mashing them slightly to mitigate that problem. But if you live for adventure, just forget about that step and leave them whole. Uncork a younger, lighter Tempranillo from Rioja or Ribera del Duero to complement the assertive flavors here.

2 tablespoons olive oil

1 small onion, diced

3 garlic cloves, minced

$1/2$ pound sweet or spicy Spanish chorizo, diced

1 pound baby spinach leaves

$1/4$ cup chicken stock or broth, or water

1 (15-ounce) can chickpeas, drained and rinsed

$1/2$–1 teaspoon sweet or spicy pimentón, or paprika

Salt and freshly ground black pepper

1 baguette, cut diagonally and baked into crostini (see page 31)

Extra virgin olive oil (preferably Spanish), for drizzling

Minced fresh flat-leaf parsley, for garnish

Heat 2 tablespoons oil in a large, heavy pot over medium heat. Add onion and sauté until softened and golden brown, about 10 minutes. Add garlic and sauté until fragrant, about 30 seconds. Add chorizo and cook until slightly crispy and fat is rendered, about 5 minutes. Add spinach and stock and sauté until spinach is wilted and dark green. Add chickpeas and $1/2$ teaspoon pimentón and cook to heat through, pressing down on chickpeas with potato masher to smash slightly. Season with salt and pepper, adding additional pimentón if desired. Spoon mixture into a serving bowl. Drizzle with extra virgin olive oil and sprinkle with parsley. Arrange toasted bread on a platter and serve.

# Fried Eggplant with Honey and Mint

## MAKES 4 MONTADITOS

*Berenjenas con miel*, as this dish is called in Spanish, is a tapas specialty of the southern region of Andalucía, where the inclusion of honey and mint reflects the influence that the Moors had on the cuisine of the area, which they ruled for centuries. This is surprisingly delicious on toast and makes a lovely starter or lunch or supper dish. Soaking the eggplant in milk helps remove any bitterness and helps prevent the eggplant from absorbing too much oil. You will want to pour a young, ripe red Garnacha, particularly from the wine regions of Campo de Borja, Somontano, or Terra Alta.

1 small globe eggplant, peeled

3 cups (about) milk

Vegetable or canola oil, for frying

1 cup (about) all-purpose flour

Salt and freshly ground black pepper

4 large, thick slices country bread

$^1/_4$ cup aromatic honey

2 tablespoons chopped fresh mint, for garnish

Trim ends off eggplant. Cut eggplant into 8 slices $^1/_4$ to $^1/_3$ inch thick. Arrange eggplant in a baking dish and pour over enough milk to cover. Let stand for 1 hour.

Pour in enough oil to come 1 inch up the sides of a large, heavy skillet. Set over medium heat until oil quickly browns a small piece of bread. Place flour on a large plate and season generously with salt and pepper. Remove eggplant slices one at a time from milk (do not dry) and dredge well in flour, shaking off excess. Add to oil and fry until golden brown on one side, and then turn and fry until golden brown on the other side, 4 to 5 minutes per side. Remove from oil and drain on paper towels. Sprinkle with salt.

Grill, broil, or toast bread. Arrange toasts on a platter or individual plates. Drizzle each toast with $^1/_2$ tablespoon honey and top with 2 eggplant slices, overlapping if necessary. Drizzle eggplant slices on each toast with $^1/_2$ tablespoon of honey. Garnish with mint and serve.

# Sardines and Piquillo Peppers with Garlic Mayonnaise

## MAKES 4 MONTADITOS

The piquillo pepper is grown near the town of Lodosa in the north central region of Navarra. It is picked during two harvests between September and December. After picking, the peppers are roasted over embers, peeled, seeded, and packed into jars or tins for sale around the world. This popular little pepper, whose name means "little beak"—which is appropriate given the pepper's shape—is sweet with no heat and has a distinctive flavor from the roasting. It is now readily available in most markets, but if you cannot find it, use regular roasted red peppers instead.

Sardines, both fresh and canned, are popular throughout Spain. Allioli, which here I will call garlic mayonnaise, though it technically is not, is the classic Catalan condiment. Traditionally it is made with just garlic, salt, and olive oil, but nowadays it is often made with eggs for both taste and ease. This makes about one cup, which is more than you will need for this recipe, but who doesn't want some extra garlic mayo hanging around the fridge? It's good on everything! Pair this with a zesty white Albariño from Galicia or, more daringly, a chilled Manzanilla sherry from Andalucía.

1/2 teaspoon salt

4 garlic cloves, minced

1 egg, room temperature

1 egg yolk, room temperature

1 cup extra virgin olive oil
(preferably Spanish)

4 large, thick slices country bread

2 (3.75-ounce) cans skinless,
boneless sardines packed in olive
oil, drained well

8 piquillo peppers, halved

1 small sweet white onion, cut into
very thin rings, for garnish

4 teaspoons drained capers,
for garnish

Place salt in a mortar. Add garlic. Using a pestle, smash garlic and salt into paste. (Alternatively, mince garlic and sprinkle with salt. Take blunt side of a large knife with both hands and drag sharp side of blade across garlic, holding blade at a slight angle so it presses and flattens garlic. Continue until paste forms.) Transfer garlic paste to the bowl of a food processor. Add egg and egg yolk and pulse to blend well. With machine running, add oil in a slow, steady stream and blend until sauce has emulsified. (Can be prepared 1 day ahead. Cover and refrigerate. Bring to room temperature before using. )

Grill, broil, or toast bread. Arrange toasts on a platter or individual plates. Spread each generously with garlic mayo. Divide sardines evenly among toasts. Place 4 pepper halves atop sardines on each toast. Garnish each with some onion slices and 1 teaspoon capers and serve.

# Tortilla Española with Romesco Sauce

## MAKES 8 MONTADITOS

The only thing that this Spanish potato and onion omelet has in common with the Mexican cornmeal staple is the name, which actually refers to the round shape of both items. Tortilla Española is beloved throughout Spain and can be served for breakfast, lunch, dinner, or most popularly, tapas. It is usually served room temperature, cut into wedges or squares, but sometimes shows up on bread, either atop one slice or between two. Here I have gilded the lily with fiery and nutty romesco, one of Catalunya's classic sauces, which hails from Tarragona. I will admit that my version is a bit of a cheat, as it uses an already-roasted pepper, tomato purée instead of roasted tomatoes, and omits the customary fried bread, but it is delicious nonetheless and goes fabulously with the tortilla, though purists may decry the non-traditional marriage. To drink, offer a fuller-bodied Tempranillo Crianza from Rioja or Navarra.

$^1/_2$ cup chopped jarred roasted red peppers

$^1/_4$ cup slivered almonds, toasted

$^1/_4$ cup skinned roasted hazelnuts

$^1/_4$ cup canned tomato purée

2 tablespoons chopped flat-leaf parsley

2 tablespoons sherry vinegar

1 teaspoon sweet or spicy pimentón, or paprika

1 teaspoon chile powder

3 medium garlic cloves

1 $^1/_2$ cups olive oil, divided

Salt and freshly ground black pepper

1 pound Yukon gold potatoes, peeled and very thinly sliced

1 large onion, halved and thinly sliced

6 eggs

8 large, thick slices country bread

Place the red peppers, almonds, hazelnuts, tomato purée, parsley, vinegar, pimentón, chile powder, and garlic in a food processor; pulse until finely chopped. With machine running, add ½ cup oil in a steady stream and blend until sauce comes together. Transfer romesco to a bowl. Season generously with salt and pepper. Let stand until ready to use. (Can be made several days ahead. Cover and refrigerate. Bring to room temperature before serving.)

Heat remaining 1 cup oil in a 10-inch nonstick skillet over medium heat until hot but not smoking. Add potatoes and onion. Season with salt and pepper. Cook until potatoes and onion are tender, stirring occasionally and adjusting heat so vegetables do not brown, about 20 minutes.

Crack eggs into a large bowl. Season with salt and pepper and whisk well. Using a slotted spoon, transfer potatoes and onion to eggs. Cover and refrigerate for 1 hour. (Can be prepared up to 8 hours ahead.) Transfer cooking oil to a bowl; reserve oil. Wipe out skillet.

Heat 2 tablespoons reserved cooking oil in the cleaned skillet. Pour egg mixture into the skillet and cook over low heat until sides of egg have set and middle begins to set, about 10 minutes. Place a platter as large or larger than the skillet atop the skillet and invert omelet from skillet onto platter; the cooked side will be now be up. Gently slide omelet back into the skillet with the uncooked side down and cook until that side is set, several minutes. Remove skillet from heat and let stand for several minutes. Place the same platter atop the skillet and invert omelet from skillet onto platter. Let stand until room temperature, and then cut omelet into 8 wedges. (Can be made 1 day ahead. Cover and refrigerate. Bring to room temperature before serving.)

Grill, broil, or toast bread. Arrange toasts on a platter or individual plates. Spread each toast generously with romesco. Top each with 1 wedge of tortilla and serve, passing remaining romesco separately.

# Jamón Serrano, Manchego Cheese, Quince Paste, and Spanish Mayonnaise

MAKES 4 MONTADITOS

At any tapas bar in Spain, you are sure to find Manchego cheese and Jamón Serrano, two of the country's best culinary products. Manchego, a cured sheep's milk cheese, comes from the central plains of La Mancha and is made the same way now as it has been for centuries. It has a unique flavor, a firm consistency, and a texture that is both buttery and lacy. (It is easy to find, but do not confuse it with Mexican Manchego, which is more like Jack cheese and made for melting, which Spanish Manchego is not.) In Spain, Manchego is most popular eaten sliced or cubed and is often served with quince paste, known as *dulce de membrillo*. Quince is a bright golden-yellow fruit that looks like the not-so-genetically-blessed offspring of an apple and a pear. It is super tart when eaten raw, but mellows lusciously when cooked. It is most often offered as a sweet jellied paste, which is available in most cheese stores and many supermarkets.

Jamón Serrano is a type of dry-aged Spanish ham that is produced throughout Spain, where it has been made since Roman times, if not before. Cured for at least a year, it ends up with a deeper color and flavor and firmer texture than its kissing cousin, prosciutto. I put that famous troika together with a mayonnaise I created that combines more of Spain's exports: sherry vinegar and pimentón. Pour a sturdy white Rioja or a Godello from Galicia.

1/4 cup mayonnaise

1 tablespoon Dijon mustard

1 1/2 teaspoons sherry vinegar

1 garlic clove, minced

1/4 teaspoon (or more) sweet or spicy pimentón, or paprika

Salt and freshly ground black pepper

4 large, thick slices country bread

4 large crisp Romaine lettuce leaves

8 very thin slices quince paste

16 thin shavings Spanish Manchego cheese (use a cheese shaver)

8 thin slices Jamón Serrano

Place mayonnaise, mustard, vinegar, and garlic in a small bowl and stir to blend well. Stir in 1/4 teaspoon pimentón, adding more if desired. Season Spanish mayonnaise with salt and pepper.

Grill, broil, or toast bread. Arrange toasts on a platter or individual plates. Divide Spanish mayonnaise evenly among toasts. Top each toast with 1 lettuce leaf and 2 slices quince paste. Cover each with 4 Manchego cheese shavings and top with 2 slices jamón. Serve immediately.

# Cider and Honey-Scented Onion Marmalade, Cabrales Cheese, and Hazelnuts

MAKES 20 TO 25 MONTADITOS

A pungent Spanish blue cheese, Cabrales is aged in limestone caves in the small, ruggedly beautiful northwestern region of Asturias, home to the famous Picos de Europa mountain range. The region is also famous for its apples, which are transformed into *sidra*, or hard cider, and is responsible for 80 percent of cider production in Spain. Needless to say, hazelnuts are the preferred nut of the area. These three ingredients come together beautifully in this montadito, with a little honey added for a bit of sweetness to contrast the sharpness of the cheese. If you cannot find Cabrales cheese, use any strong-flavored blue-veined cheese you like. The cheese screams for a semisweet white, but those from Spain are difficult to find; a Vouvray from France's Loire Valley will substitute nicely.

2 tablespoons olive oil

2 very large onions, halved and very thinly sliced

6 tablespoons hard or soft apple cider or apple juice

2 tablespoons apple cider vinegar

3 tablespoons honey

Salt and freshly ground black pepper

$^1/_2$ cup (about 2 ounces) crumbled Cabrales or other blue cheese

$^1/_3$ cup chopped toasted, skinned hazelnuts

1 baguette, sliced diagonally and baked into crostini (see page 31)

Heat oil in a large, heavy skillet over medium heat. Add onions and sauté until softened, about 10 minutes. Add cider and vinegar, cover, and sweat until onions are very soft, stirring occasionally, about 20 minutes. Uncover and simmer until liquid has evaporated. Stir in honey. Season with salt and pepper. Transfer to a bowl. Let cool to room temperature.

Stir cheese and nuts into onions. Arrange toasted bread on a platter. Top each with some of the onion mixture and serve.

# Garlic Shrimp

## MAKES 4 MONTADITOS

Garlic shrimp is a classic tapas dish, especially in the south of Spain. It is typically cooked and served in a small earthenware casserole, known as a *cazuela* in Spanish, accompanied by bread. Here it is served atop the bread. This recipe, inspired by one printed in *Cook's Illustrated* many years ago, is a tad more complicated than the traditional one, but you get a triple dose of garlic flavor, and that is a very good thing. If you like sherry, try a chilled Fino or Manzanilla, both of which complement seafood beautifully. Otherwise look for an Albariño, a bright and crisp white from Galicia.

1 pound uncooked medium shrimp, peeled and deveined, tails removed

8 tablespoons olive oil, divided

2 garlic cloves, minced

$1/2$ teaspoon salt

4 garlic cloves, crushed

8 garlic cloves, thinly sliced

1 bay leaf

$1/4$ –$1/2$ teaspoon crushed red pepper flakes

2 tablespoons dry sherry

4 large, thick slices country bread

Minced fresh parsley, for garnish

Combine shrimp, 2 tablespoons oil, minced garlic, and salt in a large bowl. Let stand for 30 minutes at room temperature.

Heat remaining 6 tablespoons oil in a large, heavy skillet over medium-low heat. Add crushed garlic and cook until garlic begins to brown, stirring occasionally, about 5 minutes. Remove and discard browned garlic, but leave garlic oil in the skillet.

Reduce heat to low. Add sliced garlic, bay leaf, and red pepper flakes (the amount depends on how spicy you like your food); cook until garlic is tender but not browned, about 5 minutes. Increase heat to medium-low. Arrange shrimp in the skillet in a single layer. Cook first side for 1 minute. Turn shrimp and cook second side for 1 minute. Increase heat to high, add sherry to the skillet, and cook until shrimp are cooked through, stirring or tossing shrimp in skillet constantly, about 1 minute.

Meanwhile, grill, broil, or toast bread. Arrange toasts on a platter or individual plates. Divide shrimp and sauce evenly among toasts. Sprinkle with parsley and serve immediately.

# FROM SMØRREBRØD TO SMÖRGÅS

## SCANDINAVIA

In Denmark it is *smørrebrød*, in Sweden it is *smörgås*, in Norway it is *smørbrød*, in Finland it is *voileipä*, and in Iceland it is *opna blasa samlokur*. But whatever it is called, it refers to an open-faced sandwich, Scandinavian style. The bread, usually a square or rectangular slice of dense whole-grain rye bread, is buttered then topped with any one of a number of ingredients, including meat, cured meat, fish, smoked fish, shellfish, fowl, eggs, or cheese, and typically complemented by vegetables such as cucumbers, tomatoes, or pickled beets, and an herb such as dill, parsley, or chervil. There is often a condiment such as mustard, mayonnaise, or fish spread from a tube, or a creamy dressing often made with mayonnaise and/or sour cream and flavored with a variety of ingredients.

Then there are the cooked items such as meatballs and fish cakes.

There is nothing slapdash or rustic about these artfully arranged compositions that are served forth for breakfast, lunch, a snack, or supper. The preparation and presentation of these classic open-faced sandwiches are taken very seriously indeed, with stores, cafes, and restaurants specializing in them and vying for the attention of nations filled with besotted consumers. And no matter how old and codified the tradition of assembling and consuming these kinds of sandwiches, they always look and taste thoroughly modern. Take a page from the Scandinavian playbook and serve one, two, or an array of these delightful sandwiches any time of day, or better yet, throw a smørrebrød party!

# THE BREAD

The most common bread for a Scandinavian open-faced sandwich is a thin square or rectangular slice of a sourdough rye bread filled with seeds and grains called *rugbrød* in Danish or *rågbröd* in Swedish. With no fat and little added sugar, the bread is considered to be one of the healthiest around and is absolutely beloved in its native lands. The most authentic versions of this bread are hard to get outside of Scandinavia, although some might be available via mail order or at your friendly neighborhood Scandinavian bakery, if you are lucky enough to have one.

Short of that, there are other options. I like to use the European-Style Whole Grain Bread from Trader Joe's, which is darker and coarser than what is typical but has the right size (4 x 4 inches) and thickness (quite thin) and heft (sturdy for being so slimline). The German brand Rubschlager makes a light Danish-Style Pumpernickel Bread (which actually tastes like rye) and a dark Westphalian-Style Pumpernickel Bread that have the same size and denseness as the one from Trader Joe's, while its Rye-Ola Black Rye Bread comes in a 5 x 3-inch oval.

In a pinch, you could also use any of the many Scandinavian crisp breads or cracker breads on the market made by Wasa, Ryvita, Leksands, GG, Finn Crisp, and Siljans. The bigger brands are available at most supermarkets, and others are available at specialty stores, IKEA, or by mail order.

If you have several days to devote to making rugbrød/rågbröd, you can find many good recipes online. Have fun!

# Smoked Herring Salad

## MAKES 6 OPEN-FACED SANDWICHES

Scandinavians adore herring, whether pickled or smoked, and the fish shows up on many open-faced sandwiches. You can get smoked herring just about anywhere. It has quite a strong flavor, so I think a little goes a long way, which is why I call for only one can. But if you love smoked herring, definitely use two cans. And if you don't love smoked herring, don't despair: this salad tastes delicious with canned tuna or canned salmon. And if you don't love fish at all, you can leave it out and still enjoy this dish. Try a glass of chilled aquavit with this sandwich—with a lager chaser, of course.

2 cups chopped shredded green cabbage

2 Persian or Kirby cucumbers, diced

2 hard-boiled eggs, diced

8 green onions, white and light-green parts only, minced

1 bunch dill, minced

1 bunch chives, minced

2 teaspoons grated lemon peel

1 (6.7-ounce) can smoked herring, drained

$^1/_3$ cup sour cream

$^1/_3$ cup mayonnaise

2 teaspoons Dijon mustard

1 lemon, halved

Salt and freshly ground black pepper

6 Scandinavian bread slices (see page 73)

Combine cabbage, cucumbers, eggs, onions, dill, chives, and lemon peel in a large bowl. Remove skin from herring and then flake herring into the bowl. Combine sour cream, mayonnaise, and mustard in a small bowl. Squeeze in juice from both halves of lemon or to taste. Season dressing generously with salt and pepper. Add dressing to salad and toss well. Season salad generously with salt and pepper.

Arrange bread on a platter or individual plates. Divide salad evenly among bread slices and serve.

# Roast Beef with Horseradish-Cornichon Cream

## MAKES 4 OPEN-FACED SANDWICHES

Here is my take on a classic Scandinavian sandwich offering that is sure to please meat lovers. I call for store-bought slices of roast beef, but if you have leftovers, use them by all means. This sandwich is both simple and sophisticated and works well for brunch, lunch, or supper. Adjust the level of horseradish to your taste and tolerance level. Pour a Scandinavian or German lager or lighter ale.

$1/4$ cup sour cream

1 tablespoon (or more) drained prepared white horseradish

Salt and freshly ground black pepper

6 cornichons, minced

1 tablespoon minced fresh chives

4 slices Scandinavian bread (see page 73)

2 teaspoons butter, room temperature

4 leaves butter lettuce

8 thin slices roast beef

4 thin whole slices red onion

Additional cornichons (optional)

Combine sour cream and 1 tablespoon horseradish in a small bowl. Taste and add additional horseradish if you want a stronger flavor. Season generously with salt and pepper. Stir in minced cornichons and chives. Set horseradish cream aside.

Arrange bread on a platter or individual plates. Spread each slice with $1/2$ teaspoon butter. Top each with 1 lettuce leaf. Drape 2 roast beef slices atop each lettuce leaf. Arrange rings from 1 onion slice atop each sandwich. Divide horseradish-cornichon cream among sandwiches, spooning attractively. Garnish or serve with additional cornichons.

# Roast Chicken, Asparagus, and Peas in Tarragon Cream

## MAKES 6 OPEN-FACED SANDWICHES

If Scandinavians have leftover chicken, it just may turn up in a salad with vegetables and a creamy dressing on an open-faced sandwich. This one sings of spring with asparagus, peas, and tarragon. (Make sure to cook your asparagus and peas thoroughly before using.) You could also make this sandwich with turkey if you prefer. If you cannot get tarragon, you can always use another herb you enjoy. Don't forget to start this dish an hour before you plan to serve it. Uncork a chilled Provençal rosé with this lovely sandwich.

3 cups cubed roasted or boiled
  chicken

1 small bunch asparagus spears,
  cooked and chopped

1 cup fresh or frozen peas, cooked

5 tablespoons mayonnaise

5 tablespoons sour cream

1 tablespoon Dijon mustard

2 teaspoons white wine vinegar

1 teaspoon sugar

Salt and freshly ground black pepper

2 tablespoons chopped fresh tarragon

2 teaspoons grated lemon peel

6 slices Scandinavian bread
  (see page 73)

3 green onions, trimmed lengthwise
  and minced, for garnish

Combine chicken, asparagus, and peas in a bowl. Combine mayonnaise, sour cream, mustard, vinegar, and sugar in another bowl; whisk well to blend. Season generously with salt and pepper. Stir tarragon and lemon peel into dressing. Pour dressing over chicken and vegetables. Cover and refrigerate for 1 hour.

Taste salad and adjust seasoning with additional salt and pepper. Arrange bread on a platter or individual plates. Mound salad atop each slice. Garnish with green onions and serve.

# Gravlax with Honey Mustard Dill Sauce

## MAKES 20 OPEN-FACED SANDWICHES

Gravlax is a Scandinavian specialty of dry-cured, unsmoked salmon. The main curing ingredients are salt, sugar, and dill, but every chef adds a little something different to the mix. This is my all-time favorite gravlax recipe. Gravlax is traditionally served with a mustard dill sauce, but some people prefer it with butter or crème fraîche and perhaps a few capers. Whatever you decide to put atop the bread and under the gravlax, this open-faced sandwich makes for an elegant light lunch or supper, appetizer, or hors d'oeuvre. (For the latter, serve it on cocktail rye.) This recipe makes a lot, but the gravlax keeps well and leftovers are delicious as is, in salads, or scrambled with eggs. Remember to start the curing process two days before you want to serve the salmon. Depending on the occasion, offer up Champagne or chilled aquavit with a lager chaser.

## Gravlax

4 large bunches fresh dill

1 whole skinless, boneless salmon fillet, about 2 $^1/_2$ pounds (preferably wild-caught)

3 tablespoons salt

3 tablespoons sugar

$^1/_4$ teaspoon allspice

$^1/_4$ teaspoon freshly ground black pepper

$^1/_4$ cup vodka or aquavit

## Mustard Sauce

$^1/_2$ cup honey mustard

$^1/_4$ cup distilled white vinegar

$^3/_4$ cup vegetable oil

2 bunches fresh dill, minced

Salt and freshly ground black pepper

20 slices Scandinavian bread (see page 73)

**For the Gravlax:** Arrange 2 bunches of dill in the bottom of a large baking dish. Set salmon atop dill. Whisk together salt, sugar, allspice, and pepper in a small bowl. Rub over top of salmon. Drizzle vodka over salmon. Top with remaining 2 bunches of dill. Cover with plastic wrap. Top with plates to cover the salmon. Set cans atop plates to weigh down the salmon. Refrigerate for 24 hours.

Remove plates, weights, and plastic wrap. Tilt dish and spoon liquid in corner over salmon. Cover with plastic wrap, but do not add plates or weights. Refrigerate for another 24 hours.

Remove dill from top of salmon. Transfer salmon to a cutting board. Using paper towels, wipe sugar and salt mix from salmon. Cut gravlax into paper-thin slices. Arrange slices on a platter.

**For the Mustard Sauce:** Mix mustard and vinegar in a bowl. Whisk in the oil in a steady stream. Stir in dill. Season with salt and pepper.

**For serving:** Arrange bread on a platter or in a basket. Set on a table alongside gravlax and sauce and serve.

# Potato and Shrimp

## MAKES 6 OPEN-FACED SANDWICHES

Scandinavians adore little shrimp, especially on open-faced sandwiches. In fact, shrimp sandwiches just might be the most popular kind! My recipe is typical of one you would find in Scandinavia, save for the potato, which is an interesting addition that you encounter occasionally. I love it, but you can leave it out if you'd like a lighter sandwich. While we don't have the caliber of shrimp the Scandinavians get in their cold, pure water, look for the best you can find. Offer a Scandinavian or German lager, or a wheat beer such as German Weissbier or Belgian wit with this sandwich.

6 small Yukon gold potatoes, peeled
  and cut into ¼-inch-thick slices

6 tablespoons mayonnaise

6 tablespoons sour cream

2 tablespoons Dijon mustard

1 tablespoon fresh lemon juice

6 tablespoons minced fresh dill

6 tablespoons minced red onion

Salt and freshly ground black pepper

6 slices Scandinavian bread
  (see page 73)

1 pound cooked bay shrimp, drained
  and patted dry

6 leaves butter lettuce

1 English hothouse cucumber, cut
  into 36 thin slices (you may have
  some leftover cucumber)

6 tomato wedges

6 fresh dill sprigs

Place potato slices in a pot. Cover with cold water. Bring to a boil and cook until tender; do not overcook. Drain potato slices.

Combine mayonnaise, sour cream, mustard, and lemon juice in a bowl. Add minced dill and onion and fold well. Season dressing with salt and pepper.

Arrange bread on a platter or individual plates. Spread 1 tablespoon dressing on each bread slice. Add shrimp to remaining dressing in bowl and mix well. Top each bread slice with 1 lettuce leaf. Divide the potato slices evenly atop each lettuce leaf. Cover each with 6 cucumber slices. Divide shrimp mixture evenly among slices and mound gently. Garnish each sandwich with 1 tomato wedge and 1 dill sprig and serve.

# Fish Cakes with Remoulade Sauce

## MAKES 8 OPEN-FACED SANDWICHES

Fish cakes are beloved in Scandinavia. There is no one classic recipe; some are made with white fish and some with salmon. But they are pretty much always served with a remoulade sauce, which is quite different from the version served in New Orleans. I call for a firm white fish, but if you use something drier such as tilapia, you may need to add more milk to the recipe. Why not try a young Côtes-du Rhône Blanc or an Alsatian Riesling with this dish?

## Fish Cakes

1 pound firm white fish fillets, such as cod, haddock, or halibut, patted dry and cubed

1 teaspoon salt

1 bunch chives, minced

2 tablespoons (1/4 stick) butter, melted

2 tablespoons cornstarch

1 egg

1/2 teaspoon freshly ground black pepper

1/8 teaspoon nutmeg

1/2 cup (about) whole milk

1/4 cup (1/2 stick) butter

## Remoulade Sauce

1/2 cup mayonnaise

1 tablespoon minced cornichons

1/2 tablespoon minced capers

1 teaspoon Dijon mustard

1/4 teaspoon curry powder

8 slices Scandinavian bread (see page 73)

**For the fish cakes:** Place fish in a food processor with salt and pulse to a rough paste. Add chives, melted butter, cornstarch, egg, pepper, and nutmeg; pulse to blend. Starting with 2 tablespoons, add enough milk to make a smooth, thick mixture (amount will vary depending on moistness of fish.) Transfer to a bowl.

Melt 1/4 cup butter in a large, heavy skillet over medium-high heat. Using 2 soup spoons, shape batter into 16 ovals. Add ovals to pan and cook until browned and fish is cooked through, 3 to 4 minutes per side (ovals will spread a bit during cooking). Transfer fish cakes to a platter. (Cook in two batches if necessary, using 2 tablespoons butter for each batch.)

**For the remoulade sauce:** Combine all the ingredients in a bowl.

**For serving:** Arrange bread on a platter or individual plates. Spread remoulade on each slice. Set 2 fish cakes on each slice and serve.

# Pork Sausages with Lingonberry Jam

## MAKES 8 OPEN-FACED SANDWICHES

A classic Danish sandwich features *medisterpølse*, pork sausages in casing, often served with a cucumber salad. Since it's pretty labor intensive to make those kinds of sausages, I thought I would offer up patties with all the same flavorings that go into those cased sausages, though here I pair them with lingonberry jam rather than cucumber salad, as I love the savory and sweet combination of flavors. Lingonberry jam—sometimes called lingonberry sauce or preserves—is wildly popular all over Scandinavia as an accompaniment to all manner of meat, sausages, meatballs, pancakes, and porridge. This absolutely delicious condiment can be found at gourmet supermarkets and IKEA, of course. To drink, try either a light ale or a bottle of Beaujolais Villages.

1 tablespoon butter

1 onion, finely diced

1 pound ground pork

³/4 cup cracker crumbs (from soda crackers or oyster crackers) or dry plain breadcrumbs

¹/2 cup whole milk

2 eggs, beaten to blend

1 teaspoon salt

¹/2 teaspoon ground white pepper

¹/2 teaspoon ground allspice

¹/2 teaspoon ground clove

¹/2 teaspoon ground nutmeg

¹/2 teaspoon ground ginger

2 tablespoons (or more) vegetable oil

8 squares Scandinavian bread (see page 73)

8 teaspoons butter, room temperature

8 teaspoons Dijon or German mustard

8 tablespoons lingonberry jam, sauce, or preserves

Melt butter in a small, heavy skillet over medium heat. Add onion and sauté until tender, about 10 minutes. Set aside

Place pork in a bowl. Add sautéed onion. Add cracker crumbs, milk, eggs, salt, pepper, allspice, clove, nutmeg, and ginger. Using a wooden spoon or clean hands, mix all ingredients until well blended; do not overmix. Divide mixture into 8 balls and set balls on a plate.

Heat 2 tablespoons oil in a large, heavy skillet over medium-high heat. Add balls to skillet, leaving space in between each. Using a spatula, flatten balls into patties. Cook patties until browned and crisp on first side, 4 to 5 minutes; flip patties over and cook until browned and crisp on second side, 4 to 5 minutes. Add a bit more oil if the skillet gets dry, and make sure patties are cooked through; no pink should remain.

Arrange bread on a platter or individual plates. Spread each slice with 1 teaspoon butter then 1 teaspoon mustard. Top each with 1 pork patty and 1 tablespoon lingonberry jam. Serve immediately.

# Roast Pork with Braised Red Cabbage

### MAKES 6 OPEN-FACED SANDWICHES

This is a classic Scandinavian flavor combination that often finds itself translated from the dinner plate to the open-faced sandwich. This makes for a complete knife-and-fork meal, perhaps accompanied by a cucumber salad and a cold beer. You can use the cabbage right away, but it actually tastes better if left to sit a day. Leftover pork and cabbage keep well, so make as many sandwiches as you want and save the rest. If you are short on time, you can always purchase a jar of braised red cabbage at the supermarket, but it won't taste quite as wonderful as this recipe, which is a keeper if I do say so myself. A hoppy ale or a nice Côtes-du-Rhône Rouge would go splendidly with this hearty sandwich.

1/4 cup (1/2 stick) butter

1 head red cabbage, cored and thinly sliced

1 onion, halved and thinly sliced

1 green apple, julienned

3/4 cup dry red wine

1/2 cup firmly packed light brown sugar

1/4 cup red or black currant jelly

1/4 cup apple cider vinegar

1 cinnamon stick

Pinch of ground cloves

Salt and freshly ground black pepper

1 (2-pound) boneless pork loin, tied with kitchen string and patted dry

1/4 cup plus 6 teaspoons stone-ground mustard

1 tablespoon chopped fresh rosemary

1 tablespoon chopped fresh thyme

6 Scandinavian bread slices (see page 73)

Melt butter in a large, heavy pot over medium heat. Add cabbage and stir to coat with butter and wilt slightly. Add onion, apple, wine, sugar, jelly, vinegar, cinnamon, and cloves and stir well. Season with salt and pepper. Cover and simmer until cabbage is very tender, dark purple, and shiny, stirring occasionally, about 1 1/2 hours. (Can be prepared several days ahead. Cool completely and refrigerate. Serve at room temperature or reheat if desired.)

Preheat oven to 400 degrees.

Set pork fat-side up on a rack in a roasting pan. Season pork with salt and pepper. Stir together 1/4 cup mustard and herbs in a small bowl. Rub mixture onto pork. Roast pork until meat thermometer inserted into thickest part of meat registers 140 to 145 degrees, about 40 minutes. Let stand for at least 10 minutes before slicing, or cool completely, and then slice into 1/4-inch thick slices. (Can be prepared 1 day ahead. Cool, wrap, and refrigerate. Bring to room temperature before serving.)

Arrange bread on a platter or individual plates. Spread each with 1 teaspoon mustard, top with slices of pork, spoon a generous amount of cabbage over the pork, and serve.

# Meatballs with Beet and Apple Salad

## MAKES 8 OPEN-FACED SANDWICHES

The Swedes love their *köttbullar* and the Danes love their *frikadeller*, or meatballs as we call them. For an evening meal, the Swedes enjoy them with creamy gravy; the Danes prefer them as is; but both like them sliced warm or cold atop a piece of bread. There are as many köttbullar and frikadeller recipes as there are households in Sweden and Denmark, and the meatballs can be made from different types of ground meat—beef, veal, pork—or any combination thereof. This recipe takes a bit from both countries. Condiments often include cucumber salad, pickled beets, braised red cabbage, or lingonberry jam; here I offer a beet and apple salad. These sandwiches are perfect for a hearty lunch or supper. Pour a frosty IPA (Indian pale ale).

1 cup finely chopped pickled beets, plus 1 tablespoon juice

1 cup finely chopped apple

$^1/_4$ cup finely chopped red onion

$^1/_4$ cup sour cream

Salt and freshly ground black pepper

$^1/_2$ pound ground beef (not too lean)

$^1/_2$ pound ground pork

$^1/_4$ cup whole milk

1 small onion, finely grated

1 egg, beaten to blend

$^1/_4$ cup fresh breadcrumbs

$^1/_4$ cup whole-wheat or rye flour

$^1/_4$ cup club soda

1 $^1/_2$ teaspoons salt

$^1/_2$ teaspoon freshly ground black pepper

$^1/_4$ cup ($^1/_2$ stick) butter, room temperature

8 slices Scandinavian bread (see page 73)

8 teaspoons butter, room temperature

8 leaves butter lettuce

Combine beets, beet juice, apple, red onion, and sour cream. Season with salt and pepper. (Can be made several hours ahead. Cover and refrigerate.)

Using a wooden spoon or clean hands, combine beef and pork in a mixing bowl. Add milk, onion, and egg and stir well. Add breadcrumbs, flour, club soda, salt, and pepper; stir well. Cover and refrigerate for 30 minutes.

Form meat mixture into 8 ovals. Melt ¼ cup butter in a large, heavy skillet (cast iron works well) over medium heat. Add meatballs and cook until crispy outside and no pink remains inside, about 10 minutes per side. Cool to just room temperature. Cut meatballs into thin slices.

Arrange bread on a platter or individual plates. Spread each slice with 1 teaspoon butter and top with 1 lettuce leaf. Arrange slices from 1 meatball atop each sandwich. Spoon some of the salad atop each and serve.

# Jarlsberg Cheese and Tomato with Marinated Cucumber Salad

MAKES 6 OPEN-FACED SANDWICHES

Norway's most famous culinary export is Jarlsberg. This semi-soft cow's milk cheese has a mild, buttery yet nutty flavor, a firm texture, and is delicious raw or cooked. Riddled with holes, it is similar in appearance to Swiss or Emmenthal cheese, and there is a reason for that: In the 1820s Swiss master cheesemakers visited Norway's Vestfold County and taught the locals some of the secrets to making Swiss-type cheese, and those locals promptly started making a cheese based on those instructions. While that cheese eventually stopped being produced, nostalgia for its taste remained. In 1956 some students at the Agricultural University of Norway decided to unearth the historic cheesemaking traditions of the region and marry them with modern practices. After a lot of research and experimentation, they came up with Jarlsberg.

The cheese is perfect in this simple but oh-so-tasty sandwich. Add slices of ham or roast pork if you like. The Scandinavian cucumber salad—which needs to be started several hours ahead—is a classic and delicious accompaniment. This calls for a richer lager, such as one in the Pilsner style.

1 hothouse cucumber, thinly sliced

1 tablespoon coarse salt

$^1/_2$ cup distilled white vinegar

$^1/_2$ cup sugar

2 tablespoons water

$^1/_2$ teaspoon ground white pepper

$^1/_4$ cup chopped fresh dill

6 slices Scandinavian bread (see page 73)

2 tablespoons ($^1/_4$ stick) butter, room temperature

2 tablespoons stone-ground mustard

12 slices Jarlsberg cheese

3 tomatoes, thinly sliced

Salt and freshly ground black pepper

Place cucumber in a bowl. Add coarse salt and toss well. Place a plate directly atop cucumber. Top with weight such as a can. Let stand for 2 hours at room temperature; water will exude from cucumber. Drain cucumber well and pat dry with paper towels. Return cucumber to a clean bowl.

Stir vinegar, sugar, water, and white pepper together in another bowl. Pour over cucumbers and toss well. Refrigerate for at least 2 hours so flavors will marry. Drain cucumbers and transfer to a serving bowl. Add dill and toss well.

Arrange bread slices on a work surface. Spread each with 1 teaspoon butter then 1 teaspoon mustard. Divide tomato slices among sandwiches, arranging decoratively. Top with 2 cheese slices. Season with salt and pepper. Arrange sandwiches on a platter or individual plates. Serve cucumber salad alongside.

# BUTTERBROTE AND BUTTERBRODI

## GERMANY AND RUSSIA

You may think these two countries are strange bedfellows, but when it comes to open-faced sandwiches, they are very much alike. That is because Russia imported the delicacies from Germany via Peter the Great, who did, of course, bring many more important things than sandwiches from the Western world to the motherland. So it's *butterbrot* (singular) and *butterbrote* (plural) in German and *butterbrod* (singular) and *butterbrodi* (plural) in Russian. Too bad the two country's mutual fondness for the sandwiches didn't stop them from going to war.

Butterbrote have been enjoyed in Germany since the fourteenth century. The literal translation of butterbrote is "butter bread," and as such—slices of bread spread with butter—are beloved as is, or better yet, crowned with savory ingredients such as meat, fish, fowl, cheese, vegetables, and herbs for lunch, a snack, or supper; or sweet toppings such as a sprinkling of sugar, a smear of jam, fresh fruit, or even chocolate for breakfast or a between-meals treat. While there are over three hundred types of bread in Germany, all of them delicious and any of them up to the task, the classic bread of choice is sourdough made with rye flour, and it can be toasted or untoasted.

In Russia butterbrodi are beloved for breakfast and lunch, and can be served on pumpernickel, rye, or white bread. However, when cut into nifty bite-size pieces, they are transformed into an elegant hors d'oeuvre called *butterbrodik* and are often an integral part of a sophisticated *zakuski* (an array of assorted appetizers). Of course, they are the perfect ballast for shots of vodka.

If you drop in unannounced at a Russian home, there is a good chance you will be served impromptu butterbrodi. The cook of the house will whip them up from whatever ingredients are on hand—including leftovers—but you will be none the wiser, as they will be beautiful and a perfect representation of Russian hospitality and ingenuity, not to mention a delicious taste of history.

In Germany bread is more than just a staple food at breakfast (*Frühstück*), break time (*Pausenbrot*), and supper (*Abendessen*), it is an integral part and reflection of German culture. Each region of the country produces its own kind of bread, for a staggering total of more than 300 varieties of dark and white breads and 1,200 varieties of rolls and mini breads. That's a lot of bread! Everyday breads tend to be sturdy and unrefined, using whole grains in their most unadulterated states. The most commonly used flour is rye, combined with another flour such as wheat or spelt. German breads can include oats, whole grains, seeds, cheese, meat, herbs, aromatics, and spices.

I like to use the pain de seigle (rye bread) from Le Pain Quotidien for my German butterbrote, as it's similar to the basic country rye bread that you find in Germany. It's the same shape as the pain au levain that I use for tartines (see page 13), so once again, if you use the largest slices from the center, you will want to use half slices for your sandwiches, and then as you move to the smaller slices, you can use whole slices. If you prefer bread with seeds, Le Pain's five-grain bread is awesome, and the square slices are the perfect size. The German brands Mestemacher and Feldkamp make long, thin slices of whole rye,

three-grain, pumpernickel, and sunflower seed breads (among others), which are sold in one-pound packages in the refrigerated deli sections of most supermarkets. However, there are many excellent kinds of artisan German rye and pumpernickel sold at bakeries and supermarkets.

Bread occupies the same exalted status in Russia, where there is no staple as important as bread, specifically black bread, which is the quintessential Russian bread. In times of trouble—and there have been many of those in Russia—a piece of bread has made the difference between life and death, and even to this day a surfeit of bread is a symbol of wealth and health.

The traditional Russian black bread recipe reads like a laundry list of ingredients—rye flour enriched with coffee, chocolate, fennel and caraway seeds, bran, molasses, cider vinegar, and onions or shallots—with the whole being greater than the sum of its parts. There are other simpler black breads from Russia, as well as former Soviet republics. There are lots of Russian bakeries and supermarkets with Russian foods sections where I live, so I have no problem finding Russian black bread, but use the best dark rye you can find.

# Chicken Schnitzel

## MAKES 4 BUTTERBROTE

As we all know, schnitzel—a thin piece of meat coated with flour, beaten eggs, and breadcrumbs and then fried—is a staple of German cuisine. While it is usually served on a dinner plate with a sauce or just some lemon, and a side of potatoes or spaetzle, it sometimes shows up atop bread as an open-faced sandwich. In Germany schnitzel is usually made with veal or pork, but I prefer chicken. A German lager might be the traditional beverage choice, but why not shake things up by offering a spicy red wine such as a Tempranillo from Spain or a Sangiovese from Italy?

2 whole or 4 halves boneless, skinless chicken breasts

Salt and freshly ground black pepper

Vegetable oil, for frying

$1/2$ cup all-purpose flour

1 teaspoon sweet paprika

2 eggs

1 cup plain dry breadcrumbs or panko

4 slices dark rye or pumpernickel bread

4 teaspoons butter, room temperature

4 teaspoons German brown mustard

Chopped fresh parsley, for garnish

1 lemon, cut into 4 wedges, for garnish

Place each chicken breast between 2 pieces of plastic wrap or in a large ziplock bag. Using the flat side of a meat mallet, pound chicken to a thickness of $1/4$ inch. Season chicken generously with salt and pepper.

Set a cooling rack over a baking sheet. Line another baking sheet with paper towels.

Pour oil into a large, heavy skillet to a depth of $1/2$ inch. Heat oil slowly to 375 degrees over medium heat. Meanwhile, place flour and paprika in a shallow bowl and season generously with salt and pepper. Stir with a fork to blend. Place eggs in another shallow bowl. Beat with a fork to blend. Place breadcrumbs in another shallow bowl.

Dredge 1 chicken breast in flour, shaking off excess; dredge in eggs, allowing excess to drip back into bowl; dredge in breadcrumbs, shaking off excess. Place on the rack over the baking sheet. Repeat process with remaining chicken. Add chicken to the skillet (in batches if necessary; do not crowd) and fry until golden brown and cooked through, 3 to 4 minutes per side. Transfer to paper towels.

Arrange bread on a platter or individual plates. Spread each with 1 teaspoon butter then 1 teaspoon mustard. Cut whole breasts in half; leave half breasts as is. Top each bread slice with 1 schnitzel. Garnish with parsley and lemon and serve immediately.

# Herbed Cream Cheese with Shredded Radish and Carrot Salad

## MAKES 6 TO 8 BUTTERBROTE

Germans love flavored cream cheese. They especially love to spread it on bread and eat the bread as is, or use it as a base for other ingredients. My herbed cream cheese is an homage to this affection and would win over the most discerning German cream cheese–loving palate, I am sure. And it makes a delectable bed for a little grated vegetable salad. This recipe is light, fresh, and perfect for any time of day. The recipe yield varies depending on how thick you like to shmear your cream cheese. This would be excellent with a cold bottle of a lighter Loire Valley Sauvignon Blanc such as Touraine or Cheverny.

8 ounces cream cheese, room temperature

2 tablespoons (¹/4 stick) butter, room temperature

2 tablespoons sour cream, room temperature

¹/2 cup minced fresh thyme, chives, dill, marjoram, and/or parsley or any combination thereof, divided

1 small shallot, minced

1 large garlic clove, minced

¹/2 teaspoon salt

¹/2 teaspoon freshly ground black pepper

2 carrots, peeled and grated

4 large radishes, grated

Extra virgin olive oil, for drizzling

6–8 slices dark rye or pumpernickel bread

Place cream cheese, butter, and sour cream in a bowl. Using a wooden spoon, mix until well blended. Add ¼ cup herbs, shallot, and garlic and mix until well blended. Stir in salt and pepper, adding more if desired. Let stand until ready to use. (Can be prepared 1 day ahead. Cover and refrigerate. Bring to room temperature before using.)

Place carrots and radishes in a small bowl. Drizzle with enough oil to coat. Season with salt and pepper. Toss with remaining ¼ cup herbs.

Arrange bread on a platter or individual plates. Slather cream cheese generously on each bread slice. Top each with a mound of veggie salad and serve.

# Sauerkraut, Sausage, and Cheese

## MAKES 6 BUTTERBROTE

I have combined several popular German ingredients in an open-faced sandwich that is inauthentic—at least as far as I know—but delicious. And while Germans may love sausages in rolls, I think they would find this amped-up riff completely irresistible! You can find precooked German sausages at most supermarkets, but if you cannot, feel free to use Polish kielbasa. Or if you prefer to start with uncooked sausages, boil them in beer to cook them completely, and then proceed with the recipe. Butterkäse is a mild semi-soft cow's milk cheese that is primarily produced in Germany, but is also made in Wisconsin; Tilsit is a lightly aged yet more flavorful semi-hard cow's milk cheese produced in Germany; both melt wonderfully. If you cannot find either, readily available Danish Havarti is a great substitute. Beer's the ticket here—a German Weissbier or Belgian wit would be perfect.

2 tablespoons (¹/4 stick) butter

1 large red onion, halved and thinly sliced

1 (14-ounce) can, jar, or bag sauerkraut, drained

1 tablespoon caraway seeds

Salt and freshly ground black pepper

2 tablespoons vegetable oil

6 precooked Weisswurst, Bratwurst, or Knockwurst sausages, butterflied

6 slices dark rye or pumpernickel bread

6 tablespoons German sweet mustard

6 large slices Butterkäse or Tilsit cheese

2 tablespoons minced fresh marjoram, for garnish

Melt butter in a medium-size heavy skillet over medium heat. Add onion and sauté until cooked through and slightly browned, about 10 minutes. Stir in sauerkraut and caraway seeds and cook until heated through, stirring occasionally. Reduce heat to lowest setting and keep warm, stirring occasionally. Season with salt and pepper.

Preheat broiler. Heat oil in a large, heavy skillet over medium heat. Add sausages cut side down in skillet and cook until browned on one side; then turn sausages and cook until browned on second side.

Set bread slices on a baking sheet. Spread each slice with 1 tablespoon sweet mustard. Divide sauerkraut evenly among bread slices. Set 1 butterflied sausage cut side up atop sauerkraut. Cover with cheese. Broil until cheese melts. Transfer to a platter or individual plates. Sprinkle with marjoram. Serve immediately.

# Quark and Sautéed Apples with Lemon and Thyme

## MAKES 4 BUTTERBROTE

Quark is a fresh, soft, white, creamy, unaged, and unsalted cheese similar to the French fromage blanc. A bit of a cross between cottage cheese and yogurt, it is beloved in Germany as well as the countries of eastern and northern Europe. Israel too! It is a blank canvas upon which to paint a masterpiece of sweet or savory flavors. Apples are the most popular fruit in Germany, and here I sauté them and place them atop the quark for an unusual open-faced sandwich that rocks for breakfast, brunch, lunch, supper, or a snack. I like Fuji apples and do not peel them, but use any apples you like and peel them if you wish. Quark is available in many fine supermarkets; if you cannot find it, I have listed substitutes below. Chilled Prosecco would be lovely to drink here.

$1/4$ cup ($1/2$ stick) butter

4 small apples or 2 large apples, cored, quartered, and thinly sliced

$1/4$ cup firmly packed brown sugar

$1/2$ teaspoon ground cinnamon

$1/4$ teaspoon grated nutmeg

$1/4$ teaspoon ground cloves

1 small lemon, halved

4 slices dark rye or pumpernickel bread

8 tablespoons ($1/2$ cup) quark, fromage blanc, small-curd cottage cheese, ricotta cheese, or Greek yogurt

2 teaspoons minced fresh thyme, for garnish

2 teaspoons grated lemon peel, for garnish

Melt butter in a medium-size heavy skillet over medium heat. Add apples and brown sugar and sauté until fruit is softened and caramelized, about 10 minutes. Add spices, squeeze in lemon juice, and stir to blend well.

Grill, broil, or toast the bread. Arrange toasts on a platter or individual plates. Spread each slice with 2 tablespoons quark. Divide apples among toasts, making sure to include syrup from skillet. Garnish with thyme and lemon peel and serve immediately.

# German Potatoes and Fried Eggs

## MAKES 6 BUTTERBROTE

While pan-fried potatoes German style—that means with bacon and onions—are most often an accompaniment to meat, such as schnitzel, I thought they would taste great on bread topped with a fried egg. If you like a lot of potatoes, use large Yukon golds; if you like a bit less, use medium-size ones. This is a perfect hearty breakfast sandwich of the open-faced variety. And if you like breakfast for dinner, you will love this dish! If it's drinking time when you serve this sandwich, try a German lager or British ale.

8 bacon strips, diced

1 large onion, diced

4 medium to large Yukon gold potatoes, finely diced

Salt and freshly ground black pepper

Sweet paprika

2 tablespoons (¼ stick) butter

6 eggs

6 slices dark rye or pumpernickel bread

3 tablespoons minced fresh parsley, for garnish

Place bacon in a large, heavy skillet over medium heat and cook until thoroughly cooked to desired crispiness and fat has been rendered. Using a slotted utensil, transfer bacon from skillet to paper towels. Pour all but 2 tablespoons fat from skillet; reserve fat.

Add onion to the skillet with the fat and sauté until browned and a bit crisp, about 15 minutes. Using a slotted utensil, transfer onion to a bowl. Add some of reserved bacon fat to skillet if dry. Add potatoes to the skillet in a single layer and season with salt, pepper, and paprika. Cover and cook until potatoes are browned and tender, about 20 minutes, turning potatoes halfway through cooking process and adding additional fat to skillet if dry (if potatoes do not fit in a single layer, cook in batches or divide between 2 skillets). Stir bacon and onions into potatoes and cook for about 3 more minutes. Keep warm over low heat.

Meanwhile, melt butter in a large, heavy skillet over medium-low heat. Break in eggs and cook until whites are firm but yolks are still runny, or to your desired degree of doneness. Season with salt, pepper, and paprika.

Toast bread. Arrange toasts on a platter or individual plates. Mound potatoes atop bread. Place 1 fried egg atop each toast. Garnish with parsley and serve.

# Scrambled Eggs with Sour Cream and Caviar

## MAKES 4 BUTTERBRODI

A typical Russian butterbrodi is brown bread spread with butter and mounded with caviar. That might be a bit much for some tastes, so I have mitigated things with some scrambled eggs and sour cream. Dark rye or pumpernickel bread would be excellent here but so would light rye or brioche—toasted if you so desire. I have called for salmon roe, which is readily available, reasonably priced, delicious, and pretty. However, use any kind of caviar that suits your taste and budget. This would be a splendid brunch or supper dish. It's hard to beat Champagne with this sandwich.

8 eggs

2 tablespoons half and half

Salt and freshly ground black pepper

4 tablespoons butter, room
  temperature, divided

1 small red onion, minced

4 slices dark or light rye bread,
  pumpernickel bread, or brioche

4 tablespoons sour cream

4 tablespoons salmon roe caviar

2 tablespoons minced fresh chives,
  for garnish

Crack eggs into a bowl. Add half and half. Season with salt and pepper. Using a fork or whisk, beat eggs briskly to break up yolks and incorporate half and half.

Melt 2 tablespoons butter in a medium-size heavy nonstick skillet over medium heat. Add onion and sauté until softened, about 8 minutes. Season with salt and pepper. Reduce heat to medium-low. Add eggs and cook, stirring constantly, until eggs are set but not dry. Remove from heat. Taste and adjust seasoning with salt and pepper.

Toast bread if desired. Arrange slices on a platter or individual plates. Spread each slice with ½ tablespoon of remaining 2 tablespoons butter. Divide scrambled eggs evenly among slices. Top each with 1 tablespoon of sour cream then 1 tablespoon of caviar. Sprinkle with chives, dividing evenly, and serve.

# Chopped Livers, Sautéed Onions, and Hard-Boiled Eggs

MAKES 6 BUTTERBRODI

While chopped liver has come to be associated with the traditional cuisine of Ashkenazi (Eastern European) Jews, it is actually a dish that has long been popular with the general population of Russia and even Germany. It is rich, delicious, and easy to make. I like slightly chunky chopped liver, so I fold in the onions and eggs after I purée the livers, but if you like your chopped liver smooth, you can purée everything together. If you prefer things really chunky, you can put everything in a wooden bowl and chop it together with a mezzaluna, just like in the old country! This makes about 2 cups, so it makes a generous sandwich. This is also great with cocktail rye bread or crackers. Amontillado sherry is a superb match with this luscious dish.

5 tablespoons vegetable oil, divided

3 large onions, diced

Salt and freshly ground black pepper

1 pound chicken livers, well-trimmed and patted dry

4 hard-boiled eggs, peeled and chopped

6 slices dark rye or pumpernickel bread

$^1/_4$ cup chopped fresh parsley, for garnish

Heat 4 tablespoons oil in a large, heavy skillet over medium heat. Add onions and cook until melted and browned, stirring frequently, 30 to 40 minutes. Season with salt and pepper.

Meanwhile, heat remaining 1 tablespoon oil in another large, heavy skillet over medium-high heat. Add livers, season with salt and pepper, and sauté until browned on the outside but still a bit pink on the inside, about 5 minutes. Let cool.

Transfer livers to a food processor and purée. Transfer to a bowl. Fold in sautéed onions. Fold in eggs. Adjust seasoning with salt and pepper.

Arrange bread on a platter or individual plates. Divide chopped liver among bread slices, mounding well. Garnish with parsley and serve.

# Russian Salad

## MAKES 6 BUTTERBRODI

Russian salad is one of the most traditional of all the dishes in the Russian culinary repertoire. It is an integral part of a *zakuski*, or an appetizer table, and is served on special occasions. Now it is beloved in many European countries, as well as Middle Eastern and South American ones. The original version, which contained more highbrow ingredients such as grouse and caviar, was invented in the 1860s by Lucien Olivier, a Belgian chef at the Hermitage, one of Moscow's most celebrated restaurants. His mayonnaise dressing was revered, and he kept the formula a secret. The recipe became more accessible over the years, and the one below is pretty much the way it is made today, though normally chunks of ham would be mixed into the salad rather than slices laid underneath the salad. If you do not like ham, use slices of roast chicken, turkey, or beef. If you are a vegetarian, leave out the meat entirely. If you are a vegan, leave out the meat and use vegan rather than regular mayonnaise. This makes 6 very hearty sandwiches; if you are a dainty eater, you could make 8 sandwiches. A light ale would be great with this, but so would chilled Russian vodka.

2 large carrots, peeled and diced

2 boiling potatoes, peeled and diced

1 cup frozen green peas

3 hard-boiled eggs, peeled and chopped

1/2 cup chopped cornichons or dill pickle

6 tablespoons mayonnaise

Salt and freshly ground black pepper

6 slices dark rye or pumpernickel bread

6 teaspoons Dijon mustard

6 long, thin slices ham

6 large leaves butter lettuce

6 green onions, minced, for garnish

1/4 cup minced fresh dill, for garnish

Bring a medium-size pot of water to a boil. Add carrots and potatoes and cook until tender, about 5 minutes. Drain and rinse under cold water.

Bring a small pot of water to a boil. Add peas and cook until tender, about 5 minutes. Drain and rinse under cold water.

Transfer carrots, potatoes, and peas to a large bowl. Add eggs and cornichons. Add mayonnaise and fold to combine. Season very generously with salt and pepper. (Can be prepared up to 1 day ahead. Cover and refrigerate. Let sit at room temperature slightly before serving.)

Arrange bread on a platter or individual plates. Spread each slice with 1 teaspoon mustard. Top each with 1 ham slice. Cover each with 1 lettuce leaf. Divide salad evenly among bread slices. Garnish with onions and dill and serve.

# Crab and Corn Salad

## MAKES 6 BUTTERBRODI

Russians have a special fondness for crab salad, and it is considered to be an elegant dish perfect for celebrations and special occasions. As with most Russian salads, a mayonnaise dressing is involved. Make sure to begin this lovely starter or light lunch dish at least 1 hour before you want to serve it. While the Russians would not offer this on toast, if you would like to do so, go right ahead! Either a lager or a Loire Valley Sauvignon Blanc would wash this down nicely.

$1/2$ pound lump crabmeat, picked over and shredded if necessary

1 lemon, halved

1 cup drained canned corn

1 large celery stalk, minced

1 small Persian or Kirby cucumber, minced

3 tablespoons minced red onion

1 tablespoon minced fresh dill

1 tablespoon minced fresh chives

1 tablespoon minced fresh flat-leaf parsley

$1/2$ cup mayonnaise

Salt and freshly ground black pepper

6 slices dark rye or pumpernickel bread

2 tablespoons ($1/4$ stick) butter, room temperature

Hard-boiled eggs, peeled and thinly sliced, for garnish

Sweet paprika, for garnish

Place crab in a bowl. Squeeze lemon over. Add corn, celery, cucumber, onion, dill, chives, and parsley to crab and fold gently. Add mayonnaise and fold gently to blend well. Season generously with salt and pepper. Cover and refrigerate for 1 hour to allow flavors to marry.

Arrange bread on a platter or individual plates. Spread 1 teaspoon butter on each slice. Divide crab salad evenly among bread slices, mounding generously. Garnish with slices of hard-boiled egg. Sprinkle with paprika and serve.

# Smoked Fish with Horseradish, Chives, and Lemon Butter

## MAKES 6 BUTTERBRODI

Smoked fish is a favorite in Russia and is often served atop a slice of buttered bread, sometimes with a bit of horseradish. Choose the fish that suits your taste and budget best and you won't be disappointed. This sandwich is lovely for brunch or supper, or even as an appetizer before a simple meal. To drink, fill your iced steins with a fine German lager.

6 tablespoons (³/4 stick) butter, room temperature

4 tablespoons minced fresh chives, divided

1 tablespoon prepared horseradish

1 teaspoon grated lemon peel

Salt and freshly ground black pepper

6 slices dark rye or pumpernickel bread

12 ounces smoked whitefish, sablefish, trout, or salmon

Combine butter, 2 tablespoons chives, horseradish, and lemon peel in a bowl and mix well. Season generously with salt and pepper.

Arrange bread on a platter or individual plates. Slather each slice with horseradish butter. Divide smoked fish evenly among bread slices. Garnish with remaining 2 tablespoons chives and serve.

# FROM BENEDICT TO RAREBIT

## THE BEST OF THE REST
## IN THE WEST

◇◇◇◇◇◇◇◇◇◇◇◇◇◇◇

In this chapter I offer recipes for some of the best open-faced sandwiches of Britain, America, and Mexico. In Europe there are places other than France, Italy, Spain, Scandinavia, Germany, and Russia that have interesting open-faced sandwiches, but their choices are not as extensive. While I do not include recipes from these places, their sandwiches are delicious, so if you go to the Netherlands, Belgium, Austria, the Czech Republic, Hungary, Poland, Estonia, or Latvia, for example, make sure to give them a try.

Great Britain is famous for a trio of sandwiches, including Welsh Rabbit, or Rarebit, and Beans on Toast, and I offer recipes for both. A recipe for Scotch Woodcock, toast spread with anchovy paste and topped with scrambled eggs, will have to wait for another day (or perhaps you could come up with your own).

America has a surprising number of sandwiches. One has attained national domination—Eggs Benedict, a recipe for which I have included here—while most of the others remain decidedly regional affairs. All have their caloric charms, and none are for the faint of heart or stomach. One of those is the Hot Brown from the Brown Hotel in Louisville, Kentucky, for which I have also included a recipe.

These days, modern American chefs are putting everything on toast, but the most popular toppings—at least for now—are mashed avocado and hummus, both in endless variations. And anything that can be put between two slices of bread can be put atop one, such as my favorites, tuna salad and egg salad. My recipes for all of these are instant classics, if I do say so myself!

Mexico offers up *molletes,* the ultimate in open-faced comfort food. If you have never sampled these pillows of beans and melted cheese, make sure to savor my versions.

Of course, it is not just the western world that has open-faced sandwiches. In Armenia there are *lahmajoun*; in Lebanon, *manakish*; in Turkey, *balik ekmek*; in Malaysia, *roti John* . . . but that is for a different book.

# THE BREAD

Because of the eclectic nature of this chapter, most of the recipes call for different types of bread. But whether whole grain, sourdough, brioche, English muffins or bolillos, all are readily available. However, if you would like to bake a loaf bread that would work for all the recipes in this chapter (except the molletes), including the Eggs Benedict and Hot Brown if you are willing to color a bit outside the lines, I have one for you. It also works great with most of the Scandinavian, German, and Russian recipes too.

I am not a true bread baker, rather someone who is fond of making quick breads: breads without yeast. And this is the quick bread I make the most because it is foolproof, delicious, and perfect on its own or with toppings—both simple and sublime. As a bonus, it only requires one bowl, one spoon, and one pan.

I adapted this recipe from one created by Marilyn Bright, an American-born, Dublin-based food journalist who I tapped to do an article on Irish breads when I worked at *Bon Appétit* magazine. This has been, is, and I am certain always will be, my favorite recipe for this kind of bread. So thank you, Marilyn.

# Brown Soda Bread

MAKES 1 LOAF

Butter, room temperature, for greasing pan

1 $^3/_4$ cups all-purpose flour

1 $^3/_4$ cups whole-wheat flour

6 tablespoons toasted wheat germ

$^1/_4$ cup old-fashioned oats (also called whole oats or rolled oats; do not use instant)

2 tablespoons firmly packed brown sugar

1 teaspoon baking soda

$^1/_2$ teaspoon salt

2 tablespoons ($^1/_4$ stick) unsalted butter, cut into small pieces

2 cups buttermilk

Preheat oven to 425 degrees. Generously butter 9 x 5-inch loaf pan.

Place all-purpose and wheat flours, wheat germ, oats, brown sugar, baking soda, and salt in a bowl; whisk or stir to blend well. Add butter to the bowl. Using clean fingertips or a pastry cutter, rub butter into the flour mixture until fine a meal forms. Using a large wooden spoon, gradually stir in buttermilk and mix until all flour is incorporated and soft dough forms. Transfer dough to prepared pan.

Bake until top of bread is dark brown and a toothpick inserted into the center comes out clean, about 40 minutes. Immediately turn bread out onto a cooling rack. Cool completely before slicing. (Can be made several days ahead. Wrap well and store at room temperature; if hot and humid, refrigerate.)

# Classic Eggs Benedict

## MAKES 4 WHOLE OR 8 HALF MUFFINS

It is crazy to mess with success, and this recipe has been a success since it was invented at the Waldorf Astoria Hotel in 1894, or so said a Wall Street stockbroker named Lemuel Benedict in an interview with *The New Yorker* magazine in 1942. He recounted how he had a terrible hangover and wandered into the hotel seeking a culinary cure. He ordered buttered toast, poached eggs, crisp bacon, and a side of hollandaise sauce. When Oscar Tschirky, the famous maître d'hôtel, heard about the combo, he decided to add it to the menu with a few substitutions: he called for an English muffin rather than toast, and a round of ham rather than strips of bacon. There are at least three other plausible stories for the origin of this dish, but none are as much fun as this one. No matter how the dish was born, the important thing is that it has endured with nary a change. It is still decadent, still delicious, and still a fabulous hangover cure. There is no question: Bloody Marys are a must!

2 teaspoons white wine vinegar

4 large egg yolks

2 tablespoons fresh lemon juice

1 teaspoon Dijon mustard

3 drops hot sauce, such as Tabasco (optional)

12 tablespoons (1 1/2 sticks) butter, melted

Salt and white pepper

8 large eggs

8 slices Canadian bacon

4 English muffins, halved

3 tablespoons butter, room temperature

Sweet paprika, for garnish

1 bunch chives, minced, for garnish

Line a platter with paper towels. Fill a large, heavy skillet with enough water to come ¾ of the way up sides of skillet. Add vinegar to water and bring to a simmer over medium-high heat.

Meanwhile, place yolks, lemon juice, mustard, and hot sauce in a blender and purée. Add a drizzle of melted butter and purée. Continue adding melted butter a little at a time, puréeing after each addition, until sauce is completely emulsified. Season hollandaise sauce with salt and pepper. Cover blender with a towel to keep sauce warm.

When water is just simmering, quickly but gently break eggs into water around the edge of the skillet. Reduce heat to medium-low and simmer until eggs are just set, about 3 minutes; do not overcook. Using a slotted utensil, transfer eggs to prepared platter. Using scissors, trim uneven edges from eggs if desired.

Place bacon in a medium-size heavy skillet and heat thoroughly on both sides. Toast English muffins and place 2 halves on each plate. Spread a generous 1 teaspoon butter on each muffin half. Top with 1 bacon round and 1 poached egg. Spoon sauce over top. Garnish with paprika and chives. Serve immediately.

# The Hot Brown

This legendary open-faced turkey and Mornay (cheese) sauce sandwich originated at the Brown Hotel in Louisville, Kentucky, during the Roaring Twenties. Back then more than a thousand guests would show up nightly for the hotel's famous dinner dance. As the sun came up and the guests got tired of doing the Charleston, they would head to the restaurant to get something to eat. Ham and eggs were the traditional offering, but Chef Fred Schmidt wanted to present something more original and delectable for his exacting clientele. And so he created the Hot Brown. It was popular then and remains popular now and is served in every eating venue at the hotel. In the hotel's classic recipe, the Mornay sauce is made with heavy cream; I prefer to make it with milk. This sandwich is delicious any time of the day or night and goes really well with a chilled beer. Why not try your favorite local microbrew?

$1/4$ cup butter

$1/4$ cup all-purpose flour

2 cups whole milk

Salt and freshly ground black pepper

Freshly grated nutmeg

$3/4$ cup grated Pecorino Romano cheese, divided

$1/2$ cup grated sharp white cheddar cheese

4 thick slices brioche, challah, white sandwich bread, or Texas toast

1 pound thinly sliced turkey

2 large tomatoes, thinly sliced

Sweet paprika, for garnish

2 tablespoons chopped fresh parsley, for garnish

8 bacon slices, cooked until crispy

Preheat broiler.

Melt butter in a medium-size heavy saucepan over medium heat. Whisk in flour and continue whisking until roux just begins to brown, about 2 minutes. Whisk in milk and bring to a boil, whisking constantly. Reduce heat and simmer until sauce is thickened, whisking frequently, about 5 minutes. Remove from heat. Season sauce to taste with salt, pepper, and nutmeg. Stir in $1/2$ cup Pecorino Romano and the cheddar cheese.

Set each bread slice in an individual gratin dish or on an ovenproof plate, or arrange bread slices on a broiler pan or baking sheet. Divide turkey slices evenly among bread. Divide tomato slices evenly among bread. Spoon sauce over sandwiches, dividing evenly. Sprinkle each with some of the remaining $1/4$ cup Pecorino Romano.

Broil until tops are golden brown, about 5 minutes. If using a broiler pan or baking sheet, transfer each sandwich to a plate. Sprinkle with paprika. Divide parsley among sandwiches. Cross 2 pieces of bacon across each sandwich and serve immediately.

# Curried Egg Salad with Mango Chutney, Raisins, and Cashews

### MAKES 4 TOASTS

Egg salad is an open-faced sandwich favorite all over the Western world, and I love it in every rendition. This one is a takeoff of one of my favorite chicken salads. I line the bread with watercress for some color and crunch, but if you can't find it, use baby spinach leaves instead. I prefer Major Grey's chutney, which is a type of chutney rather than a brand, and is made by several manufacturers, but feel free to use whatever mango chutney you like. Try this for brunch, lunch, or supper. Pair this with a bone-dry white Kerner from the Alto Adige in Italy.

6 hard-boiled eggs, peeled

$1/4$ cup mango chutney, preferably Major Grey's

$1/4$ cup mayonnaise

$1/4$ cup minced celery

3 tablespoons golden raisins

2 tablespoons minced green onion

1 teaspoon yellow curry powder

Salt and freshly ground black pepper

4 slices whole-wheat or whole-grain sandwich bread

1 bunch watercress, tender stems and leaves only

4 tablespoons chopped roasted, salted cashews

Chop eggs and place in a bowl. Add chutney, mayonnaise, celery, raisins, green onion, and curry powder; mix well. Season generously with salt and pepper. Cover and refrigerate for 1 hour to meld flavors.

Toast bread. Arrange toasts on a platter or individual plates. Line each toast with watercress. Mound egg salad atop watercress. Sprinkle 1 tablespoon cashews over each toast and serve.

# Traditional Molletes with Pico de Gallo

## MAKE 4 WHOLE OR 8 HALF MOLLETES

Toasted bread with refried beans, melted cheese, shredded lettuce, and pico de gallo salsa: how could anything be more satisfying, not to mention filling? No wonder molletes are a Mexican favorite all over the country and are offered on almost every breakfast menu. This one is the classic and is delicious as is, but you can easily dress it any way you like: add ham, chorizo, bacon, or mushrooms; top it with guacamole or crema. If you cannot find Mexican cheese, use Monterey Jack or domestic fontina. Don't forget to make the salsa at least 1 hour ahead. This dish calls for a cold Mexican beer. If you can find one of the fabulous microbrews coming out of Baja, try one; otherwise, grab a Bohemia or Modelo Especial and you won't be disappointed.

2 pounds ripe Roma or plum tomatoes, halved, seeded, and chopped

1 large white onion, minced

1 bunch cilantro, leaves finely chopped

4 serrano chiles, seeded, deveined, and minced

2 limes, halved

Salt and freshly ground black pepper

4 bolillos, teleras, pan francés, French rolls, Kaiser rolls, or ciabatta rolls

4 tablespoons (1/2 stick) butter, room temperature

1 (31-ounce) can or 2 (15- to 16-ounce) cans refried beans

1 1/2 cups grated Mexican melting cheeses, such as Oaxaca, asadero, Chihuahua, Manchego (not Spanish), or any combination thereof

1 head iceberg lettuce, cored and shredded, for garnish

Combine tomatoes, onion, cilantro, and chiles in a bowl. Squeeze juice from lime halves over mixture then season with salt and pepper. Toss well. Let pico de gallo stand for at least 1 hour; do not refrigerate.

Preheat broiler. Cut each roll in half, but do not cut all the way through. Scoop out and discard insides of roll, leaving a 1/2-inch-thick shell. Spread 1/2 tablespoon butter on each roll half. Arrange rolls on broiler pan or baking sheet. Broil until crispy. Remove from broiler.

Place beans in a medium-size heavy saucepan. Add a little water to thin, and stir to heat through. Spoon beans onto roll halves, dividing evenly. Sprinkle rolls with cheese, dividing evenly. Broil until cheese melts, 1 to 2 minutes. Transfer each mollete to a plate. Garnish with lettuce. Serve immediately with pico de gallo.

# Molletes with Black Beans and Rajas

## MAKES 4 WHOLE OR 8 HALF MOLLETES

The classic refried pinto bean, cheese, and salsa mollete provides inspiration for many variations, including this one. Here black beans are lightly refried, placed atop the butterflied roll, and then topped with *rajas*, one of Mexico's easy yet elegant culinary stars: roasted poblano chiles sautéed with cream and cheese. Roasting and peeling the poblanos is a bit of a pain but totally worth it. A chilled Mexican beer is the perfect beverage choice, perhaps a microbrew from Baja. One hundred percent agave tequila would be delicious too.

6 fresh poblano chiles

1 tablespoon vegetable oil

1 small onion, chopped

3 large garlic cloves, minced

1 (15- to 16-ounce) can black beans with liquid

$^1/_2$–1 cup water

Salt and freshly ground black pepper

6 tablespoons ($^3/_4$ stick) butter, room temperature, divided

1 large onion, halved and thinly sliced

1 cup Mexican crema, sour cream, or crème fraiche

1 cup grated Mexican melting cheeses, such as Oaxaca, asadero, Chihuahua, Manchego (not Spanish), or any combination thereof

4 bolillos, teleras, pan francés, French rolls, Kaiser rolls, or ciabatta rolls

1 bunch cilantro, chopped, for garnish

Preheat broiler. Arrange chiles on a broiler pan or baking sheet and broil until blackened on all sides, using tongs to turn chiles frequently. Alternatively, place chiles directly over open flame on stovetop and grill until blackened on all sides, using tongs to turn chiles frequently. Transfer to a bowl. Cover with plastic wrap and let stand until skins loosen, about 15 minutes. Rub and/or peel skin off of chiles. Cut chiles open. Using a small, sharp knife, remove veins and seeds. Cut chiles into thin strips. Set aside. (Can be prepared 1 day ahead. Cool, cover, and refrigerate.)

Heat oil in a medium-size heavy skillet. Add chopped onion and sauté until softened, about 5 minutes. Add garlic and stir until fragrant, about 30 seconds. Add beans with their liquid. Using a potato masher, mash beans to create a coarse purée and heat through, stirring in water to make beans creamy. Season with salt and pepper. Keep warm over very low heat.

Melt 2 tablespoons butter in a large, heavy skillet over medium heat. Add sliced onion and sauté until softened, about 10 minutes. Add chiles and cook until tender, about 10 minutes. Stir in crema and heat through. Stir in cheese and cook until melted. Season rajas with salt and pepper.

Preheat broiler. Cut each roll in half, but do not cut all the way through. Scoop out and discard insides of roll, leaving a $^1/_2$-inch-thick shell. Spread $^1/_2$ tablespoon butter on each roll half. Arrange on a broiler pan or baking sheet. Broil until crispy. Remove from broiler and transfer each roll to a plate. Spoon beans into each roll half. Spoon rajas atop beans. Garnish with cilantro and serve.

# Welsh Rarebit

## MAKES 6 RAREBITS

This beloved British dish, originally called Welsh Rabbit, is basically a revved-up melted cheese sauce poured over toast. The first recorded reference of this classic tavern supper offering was in 1725, but the exact origin is unknown, and there are at least three theories floating around. In terms of the name, the grammarian H.W. Fowler opines in his 1926 edition of the *Dictionary of Modern English Usage*: "Welsh Rabbit is amusing and right. Welsh Rarebit is stupid and wrong." Or as it is more politely put in the *Oxford English Dictionary*, Welsh rarebit is an "etymologizing alteration. There is no evidence of the independent use of rarebit." Be that as it may, it seems that rarebit has stuck, but no matter what you call it, the dish is an object lesson in decadent lusciousness. Be generous with the sauce and make sure to offer knives, forks, and even spoons—no one will want to miss a drop! When in Wales . . . it's Felinfoel Double Dragon Ale, of course!

$^1/_4$ cup ($^1/_2$ stick) butter

$^1/_4$ cup all-purpose flour

4 teaspoons Worcestershire sauce

1 tablespoon Dijon mustard

$^1/_2$ teaspoon salt

$^1/_2$ teaspoon freshly ground black pepper

1 cup dark beer

1 $^1/_2$ cups heavy cream

12 ounces sharp cheddar cheese, grated

Hot sauce, such as Tabasco

6 large slices wheat or whole-grain bread

Minced fresh parsley, for garnish

Melt butter in a medium-size heavy saucepan over medium heat. Whisk in flour and continue whisking until roux is golden brown, 2 to 3 minutes. Whisk in Worcestershire sauce, mustard, salt, and pepper. Add beer and whisk until smooth. Add cream and whisk until smooth. Gradually add cheese, whisk, and cook until all cheese melts and sauce is smooth, about 5 minutes. Remove from heat and whisk in hot sauce to taste. Adjust seasoning with additional salt and pepper.

Meanwhile, grill, broil, or toast bread. Set each toast on an individual plate. Divide rarebit evenly among toasts. Garnish with parsley and serve.

# Beans on Toast

## MAKES 6 TOASTS

If you have ever spent a significant amount of time in England, then you probably know about—and perhaps have eaten—beans on toast. It is a classic dish made with canned small white beans in tomato sauce, most often the Heinz brand. The blue-labeled can is an iconic British product and can be purchased online, at Walmart, or at Cost Plus World Market, not to mention British specialty stores and some supermarkets. Heinz invented this dish in the late 1920s as a marketing tool, and not a moment too soon, it seems, as it ended up becoming an essential part of the English culinary repertoire in the post-war era, when hard times and rationing were in place. Beans and bread were often all people could afford, and the marriage of the two made for a nutritious and filling meal. Believe it or not, the dish is still popular today. In my version I add a host of ingredients to amp up the flavor profile. The vinegar and mustard lend quite a kick; if you want things a bit more subtle, just cut those amounts in half. And yes, the beans are meant to spill over the toast. And yes, you must eat this with a knife and fork, pushing the beans on the toast and the fork with your knife, just as they do in Dear Old Blighty. To drink: a pint of bitter, please!

2 tablespoons vegetable oil

1 large onion, diced

2 large garlic cloves, minced

2 (13.7-ounce) cans Heinz Beans in Tomato Sauce

2 tablespoons firmly packed brown sugar

2 tablespoons molasses

2 tablespoons Worcestershire sauce

2 tablespoons apple cider vinegar

2 teaspoons mustard powder

Salt and freshly ground black pepper

6 thick slices sourdough bread

1 cup grated cheddar cheese

Chopped fresh parsley, for garnish

Heat oil in a large, heavy skillet over medium heat. Add onion and cook until softened but not browned, stirring frequently, about 10 minutes. Add garlic and sauté until fragrant, about 30 seconds. Stir in beans, sugar, molasses, Worcestershire sauce, vinegar, and mustard; simmer until slightly thickened and flavors have married, 8 to 10 minutes. Season with salt and pepper.

Grill, broil, or toast bread. Set each piece of toast on an individual plate. Divide beans evenly among toasts. Divide cheese evenly among toasts. Garnish with parsley and serve.

# Tuna Fish Salad

## MAKES 4 TOASTS

I love tuna fish salad on its own, pressed between two pieces of squishy bread, or mounded atop toast. It is incredibly satisfying and filling and always makes me happy. While I am open to every newfangled incarnation of the salad that I have tasted in restaurants across the country, I am partial to the old-fashioned version with which I grew up. Here it is. (If you are not a fan of sweet pickle relish, you can leave it out or substitute an equal amount of dill pickle relish.) My mom used to serve this to me with a glass of ice-cold skim milk; at summer camp it was accompanied by the infamous "bug juice." But now I would suggest a local IPA (Indian pale ale) in a frosty glass.

2 (6-ounce) cans water-packed tuna, drained

2 hard-boiled eggs, peeled and chopped

$1/2$ cup mayonnaise

$1/2$ cup minced celery

$1/4$ cup minced red onion

2 tablespoons sweet pickle relish

1 tablespoon fresh lemon juice

Salt and freshly ground black pepper

4 slices whole-wheat or whole-grain sandwich bread

4 large leaves romaine lettuce, halved, or 8 small leaves romaine lettuce

Place tuna in a bowl and flake with a fork. Add eggs, mayonnaise, celery, onion, relish, and lemon juice and mix well. Season generously with salt and pepper.

Toast bread. Arrange toasts on a platter or individual plates. Top each toast with 2 large lettuce leaf halves or 2 small lettuce leaves. Divide salad among toast slices, mounding gently. Serve immediately.

# Hummus with Greek Salad and Yogurt

## MAKES 6 TOASTS

I usually eat and offer hummus as a dip, but it rocks on an open-faced sandwich. This one is easy, colorful, healthful, and delicious and is perfect for any time of day. I know that Greek salads have feta cheese, but this one doesn't as I call for a dollop of Greek yogurt on top instead. If you want to make your own hummus, either from dried or canned chickpeas, go for it, but I find that there are so many great brands on the market that I tend to buy an already-prepared version. This sandwich calls for the earthy minerality of a white wine from Campania such as Falanghina, Greco di Tufo, or Fiano di Avellino.

2 cups shredded romaine lettuce

2 Persian or Kirby cucumbers, chopped

2 plum tomatoes, seeded and chopped

2 green onions, halved vertically and minced

$1/4$ cup chopped pitted Kalamata or other Mediterranean black olives

2 tablespoons minced fresh dill, plus more for garnish

2 garlic cloves, minced

Salt and freshly ground black pepper

2 tablespoons red wine vinegar

$1/4$ cup olive oil

6 thick slices whole-wheat, whole-grain, or sourdough bread

12 tablespoons hummus

6 tablespoons Greek yogurt

Combine lettuce, cucumbers, tomatoes, green onions, olives, and 2 tablespoons dill in a bowl. Place garlic in another bowl. Season garlic generously with salt and pepper and stir with a fork. Stir in vinegar. Whisk in olive oil. Pour over salad and toss well.

Grill, broil, or toast bread. Arrange toasts on a platter or individual plates. Spread each toast with 2 tablespoons hummus. Spoon salad atop hummus, and dollop with 1 tablespoon yogurt. Garnish with dill and serve.

# Jill's Avocado Toasts

MAKES 4 TOASTS

I cannot eat avocados. No need to detail what happens if I do, but suffice it to say that this California girl has never known the glories of guacamole, many salads and sushi rolls, and of course, the latest favorite in the world of open-faced sandwiches: avocado toast. As luck would have it, my sister, Jill, a fantastic cook and an avocado aficionado, offered to create an avocado toast recipe for me. In it the rich green fruit is complemented by fennel, feta cheese, and microgreens. It is important that the fruit you select be just ripe and not underripe or overripe. And yes, of course, the recipe has been tested. Twice. Just not by me! Choose a Friulian Pinot Grigio to accompany this modern classic.

2 just-ripe avocados

1 lemon, halved

Salt and freshly ground black pepper

Hot sauce, such as Tabasco

4 thick slices whole-wheat, multigrain, or sourdough bread

Extra virgin olive oil, for drizzling

Sea salt

2 fennel bulbs, trimmed, cored, and thinly sliced

$^1/_2$ cup crumbled full-fat feta cheese, for garnish

$^1/_2$ cup microgreens, for garnish

Remove pit from avocado, place flesh in a bowl, and mash gently. Squeeze in lemon juice to taste. Season generously with salt and pepper. Mix in as much hot sauce as you desire.

Grill, broil, or toast bread. Drizzle with olive oil and sprinkle with sea salt. Arrange toasts on a platter or individual plates. Divide mashed avocado evenly among toasts. Divide fennel among toasts, arranging slices artfully across avocado. Garnish each toast with 2 tablespoons feta cheese and 2 tablespoons microgreens. Serve immediately.

# ACKNOWLEDGMENTS

First I must thank my literary agent, Deborah Ritchken, who is also a cherished longtime friend. Her love, encouragement, support, and determination made this book a reality. I do not know what I would do without her in both my personal and professional life.

Next I must thank my amazing and talented husband and daughter, Craig and Clara Plestis, who are my best cheerleaders, taste testers, and technical advisors. The two of you are life's greatest gifts. I am not sure what I did to deserve you, and I cannot imagine my life without you. You inspire me every day in ways big and small.

Big thanks to my brilliant sister, Jill Sandin, who is always there for me and has more faith in me than I have in myself; and to her equally brilliant husband, Chris Sandin, who did the stellar wine and spirits notes for this book. We have shared so much in this life; here's to much more.

To my fabulous friends—you know who you are—you keep me happy and sane and mean more to me than words can ever express. Here's a special shout-out to Carrie Kane in New York, who has been my friend longer than anyone else. Your unconditional love, compassion, sage advice, and positive outlook have been essential to my survival. Another shout-out goes to cookbook author and cooking teacher extraordinaire Susan Herrmann Loomis in France. We met at La Varenne in Paris long ago and have been laughing and crying at the vagaries of life ever since.

This book would not have happened without the talented recipe testers in the US and Canada who gave so generously of their time and expertise to test my recipes. My thanks to, in alphabetical order: Chef Kristy Stephens Ammann, Robin Beckett Currie, Christine Dutton, Jenny Hartin, Sandy Kitchen, Sita Krishnaswamy, Rochelle Rashotsky, Vivan Savares, Fern Spierer, and Karen S. Wirima. You are the best and I could not have done it without you!

And last, but certainly not least, here's to my editor, Kerry McShane, and the entire team at Gibbs Smith. Thanks for everything.

I began the book with a dedication to my parents, Leanore and Arthur Saltz, and I will end it with one as well. There is no me without you. *Merci.*

# ABOUT THE AUTHOR

Karen Kaplan is a freelance writer, editor, translator and recipe developer. She was on staff at *Bon Appétit* for twenty years and helmed the only issue of the publication to win a National Magazine Award when it was based in Los Angeles. She was also the restaurant critic for the *L.A. Weekly*, a radio host, a consultant for culinary websites and food-based reality television shows, a contributor to food and travel magazines, and a writer and recipe editor for several major cookbooks. She holds Le Grand Diplôme d'Etudes Culinaires from La Varenne Ecole de Cuisine, has taught at USC and UCLA, and speaks Spanish, French, and Italian. She lives in Studio City, California.

# INDEX

# METRIC CONVERSION CHART

| VOLUME MEASUREMENTS | | WEIGHT MEASUREMENTS | | TEMPERATURE CONVERSION | |
|---|---|---|---|---|---|
| U.S. | Metric | U.S. | Metric | Fahrenheit | Celsius |
| 1 teaspoon | 5 ml | ½ ounce | 15 g | 250 | 120 |
| 1 tablespoon | 15 ml | 1 ounce | 30 g | 300 | 150 |
| ¼ cup | 60 ml | 3 ounces | 85 g | 325 | 160 |
| ⅓ cup | 80 ml | 4 ounces | 115 g | 350 | 175 |
| ½ cup | 125 ml | 8 ounces | 225 g | 375 | 190 |
| ⅔ cup | 160 ml | 12 ounces | 340 g | 400 | 200 |
| ¾ cup | 180 ml | 1 pound | 450 g | 425 | 220 |
| 1 cup | 250 ml | 2¼ pounds | 1 kg | 450 | 230 |

# Haiti